THE FINANCIAL FREEDOM BOOK

D. MELIK MONAL

TESTIMONIALS

“

I was able to build a tax empire through the mentorship of Mr. Monal. During the mentorship I have had the added bonus of learning some of the many financial freedom hacks that the wealthy use every day.

This book is worth the investment as you are gaining years of financial knowledge and acumen, laid out in an easy to execute format.

JENNIFER RODRIGUEZ
Owner, Platinum Taxes

“

Melik has changed my life with his knowledge of how money works and how to achieve Financial Freedom. Within 5 years he has recalibrated my mindset. Following his financial plan, I am now the proud owner of two tax offices, and on path to be a 7 figure earner before I’m 32. I owe it all to Melik “Mr. Blueberry” Monal. I am confident that The Financial Freedom Book will change many lives.

CHRISTOPHER J. DESROSIERS
Entrepreneur

THE FINANCIAL FREEDOM BOOK

D. MELIK MONAL

Staleon Group
Publications | St. Louis • Orlando

THE FINANCIAL FREEDOM BOOK

First Edition
ISBN-13: 978-0-615-51655-4

Printed in the United States of America.

Published by:
STALEON GROUP PUBLICATIONS
10524 Moss Park Rd,
STE 204, PMB 342
Orlando, FL 32832
www.StaleonPublishing.com

MONAL CAPITAL
& FINANCIAL SERVICES

Table of Contents

Dedication

DEDICATON

A tribute to my parents, Jyolette Meide and Dicadieu Monal. Rest in peace. Thank you for always believing in me and passing down a rare but distinct will and desire to be great. You both instilled something in me that cannot be duplicated.

I promise you I will create and carry on a new family legacy, to pass it down to your granddaughter, Mia-Amora Monal. She reminds me so much of you, mom, and with a heart of gold - just like you, dad. Becoming successful wasn't enough for me, so I wrote this book in dedication to each of you. Thank you for paving the way for me and allowing me to create something of such magnitude that I now instill in Mia to continue the Monal Legacy.

No one can ever understand the sacrifices you made for our family, but I do and this is why I'm dedicating my first book to you mom and dad. Life is precious and procrastination is the number one dream killer. So live life with purpose, so we're not just existing, but we're living to our full potential.

I leave you with one of your sayings, mom, "One of your biggest downfalls could be *is that you're always expecting people to treat you the way you treat them and it will never happen.*" Live on beautiful souls until we meet again.

Preface

PREFACE

Every day you get 24 hours; 1,440 minutes; 86,400 seconds to become better than you were yesterday. Be very selective of how you choose to use your time, your most valuable asset. Don't get comfortable. Think outside of the box. Understand where you are trying to go and what it takes to get there. Everything starts with you.

I don't know who needs to hear this, but every day I wake up and rely on myself. I understand that accountability is the glue that ties commitment to results. What changed my life was taking responsibility for my actions and taking ownership of my mistakes, while learning from them. Blaming is easy and taking accountability is hard. It's so easy to blame others for your shortcomings, but meeting them head-on requires a different type of mindset.

The goal is always to live your life in abundance, which generally creates happiness, while living your life on your own terms. But in order for you to do so there has to be a drastic shift in your life. You have to make a conscious decision to better your life, because no one else will. Have you ever heard that old saying, "you can lead the horses to water, but you can't make him drink it?" That's exactly how I feel about this book. I can give you the entire blueprint, step-by-step, on how I became financially free, but that doesn't mean you're going to obtain financial freedom. You have to want it for yourself. It all starts with you!

No one is coming to save YOU - your life is 100% your responsibility. Now that we're clear on that no one is saving you, who's ready to become Financially Free? Reaching financial freedom is not an easy process to accomplish. There will be obstacles, but as long as you're in the right mindset you can overcome them. Becoming financially free is more mental than anything. Becoming aligned with yourself allows you to think and process things differently.

I meditate for 10 minutes every morning before I get my day started, which helps me focus. Words of affirmation are another way of training the mind. Your morning rituals can make or break your day. Repeat after me: "I will reach financial freedom." Speaking things into existence is your first step to achieving what you desire in life. All it takes is for you to think it, say it, then do it!

Let's get to business. If you were to stop working tomorrow, how much money would continue flowing into your bank account each month? If the answer is zero, then I guess you are a part of that 95% of our population that lives paycheck to paycheck. Only 1% or maybe 1.5% has figured out the secret to the money game. Millions of Americans are confused and overworked, in a "Paid on Friday- Broke by Monday" rat race.

Not only that, 63% of Americans don't have at least $500 in their savings for an emergency. We live in a very systematic country. In order for you to reach any type of success, you have to learn the system and most importantly, change your mindset. Like Uncle Steve Harvey said, "you have to get comfortable with being uncomfortable, because obtaining success or financial freedom is not a comfortable process." You have to be willing to do extra to get ahead of those who are comfortable being ordinary. Not to say being ordinary is a bad thing, but from experience, success doesn't come from being ordinary. You have to be willing to do things that the 99% won't do in order to become that 1%.

Sacrifice, commitment and long hours of hard work and dedication. A lot of us choose to sleep and procrastinate while life passes by, but like the bible says, "he who loves to sleep in the folding of hands, poverty will set upon you like a thief in the night." So, it's safe to say success loves speed and taking advantage of the time we have now is a necessity.

It's time to take action. While they sleep you should work. While they party, you should build. What excuses are you willing to let go to get to the next level of your life? Surround yourself with like-minded individuals who can help you move toward in life.

I wrote this book to not only inspire, but actually help those individuals who are looking to gain financial freedom, success and building a legacy! If these are not your aspirations, the information given in my book may not be for you.

Introduction

INTRODUCTION

I Am Mr. Blueberry

I was born in a small poverty-stricken town in Florida called Belle Glade, where financial literacy was nonexistent. My parents were immigrants from Haiti. They came to the United States in search of a better life. My mother and father, who both worked as migrant workers, chose to do what was fit to provide for our family. Working long hours in an unbearable working environment came second nature to my parents, coming from Haiti. Although my parents were amazing their lives were short-lived. Consider yourself lucky if both your parents are still here today.

I lost both of my parents very early in life, which had a huge effect on my life. But it didn't stop me, it gave me a new sense of purpose and a will to be great! Growing up in poverty, many would say it was a disadvantage, but I beg to differ. Although it was difficult, I was always taught to live life in perspective and how to pull something positive from every negative situation. I felt I had an unfair advantage. I gained instincts, street-smarts and a strong desire for success. These are some traits and characteristics I feel can't be taught- you only can adapt to within your environment.

I am Mr. Blueberry. As a teen, my entire family and I would travel north to Hammonton, New Jersey (the blueberry capital of the world) every summer to earn money picking blueberries. This is where I gained the name, Mr. Blueberry. Although I hate the smell and taste of blueberries, looking back now, I realize why. Working in the harsh conditions of those farms created my love \ hate relationship with blueberries. Looking back at it now, it's pretty funny. Most parents wouldn't allow their children to work in in such a harsh environment, but my mother had her reasons. What I gained from working in those summers were priceless. I learned the true definition of hard work. Nothing is given - everything is earned. I honestly believe I am the man I am today because of the path my mother paved for me. Now as a successful businessman and entrepreneur I have positioned myself to pass on what I've learned and how I became financially free... from blueberries to riches.

Mindset

Most of those who have achieved greatness have been told at least once in their life that it wasn't possible. Many were told that they would never amount to anything. But they believed that they could achieve anything, and worked hard to do so. On the other hand, some people will never achieve success because they're not aligned with themselves. They have no ambition, goals or desire to win. The truth is, if you want to be great in this life, you have to model that greatness in your thinking. You have to think it before you can achieve it and celebrate it. Only then will you be in the right mindset to enact change in our culture. When building a certain mindset, you must first have goals outside of your comfort zone that will challenge you. In order for you to do something you've never done; you have to become somebody you've never been.

Your attitude determines your destination. Speaking things into existence and having a positive outlook on life can help you become greater than you could ever imagine. Your mindset is the key to your success. It all starts with you asking yourself what category would you place yourself in. Who are the people that you spend most of your time with? Most importantly, what's fueling you to be better? What's your why?

Don't be afraid to be different and speak things into existence. Like I mentioned before, growth is a very uncomfortable process. This is why so many people choose to stay the same. I've dealt with individuals who were afraid to be different because they were afraid of what people would think of them. When you stop thinking what others think of you, that's when you start living the best version of yourself. Don't be afraid to be different. Be afraid of being the same as everyone else. Live outside of the box and live up to your expectations. Before I transition into this life-changing information I purposely spent the majority of my time on the Mindset chapter. Why? Because I feel your mindset and growth is the most important key in succeeding. If your mindset isn't where it needs to be, the information provided to you in my book will simply be useless.

Being rich and successful is nothing more than mindset. If you can think it you can be it, create it and even achieve it.

Rich Mindset

In the Money Game you must do whatever it takes to get to the information. The act of not knowing can cost you a fortune. Obtaining the right information will help you avoid countless mistakes and position yourself to capitalize off life-changing investments. Always keep in mind, the majority of the time it takes money to make money. Billionaires lose millions to become billionaires. Millionaires lose thousands to become millionaires. Unfortunately, many broke individuals are not willing to lose anything, but still expect to get rich. It's all a mindset. What are you willing to sacrifice?

Where is your level of thinking? Where do you categorize yourself? Do you have an employee, business owner, self-employed, entrepreneur, or investor mindset? It's so easy to pinpoint what someone's level of thinking and mindset based on the words they chose to use when speaking on acquiring wealth or speaking in general. The rich will find a way; the poor will always find excuses.

Exchanging time for money is a nonstop cycle. Don't lose sight of your goals chasing a lifestyle or even falling victim to a systematic country. The government system wasn't created to help you build your legacy, or to use the system to your advantage. Stay in tune with yourself and align with your goals. True wealth is happiness. When you break it all down, that's what we're chasing – happiness. So, if being financially free brings me closer to happiness, I'll do whatever it takes to obtain it. The goal is to always be the best version of yourself and be happy doing it.

Credit and Debt

Growing up I was never taught how to manage or leverage credit. Before we get into the complexities of credit, I think it's wise that we understand the basics of credit. Credit is the ability to obtain goods or services before making the full payment based on the trust that payment will be made in the future. Your credit score basically helps lenders and financial institutions know how responsible you are when it comes to you managing money.

Many successful people leverage their credit to build wealth. If you learn how to acquire lines of credit and use them to your advantage you will never go broke. I like to think of it as having an endless supply of funds using other people's money (OPM). However, it is only an endless supply if you use it to your financial benefit. If you fail to do this, you will pay it back with interest. After reading my book you will know what exactly is credit, what's a credit report, and what a good credit report looks like, and how you can leverage credit to build wealth like the rich.

During my upbringing debt was always considered something bad in our household so I wanted no part of it until I understood there is also such a thing as good debt. I would equate bad debt with taking on too much risk without the ability to repay. Good debt can help borrowers accomplish an objective or help them avoid a bad outcome. In this chapter I will break down good debt scenarios and bad debt scenarios to help you identify what is needed to build residual income.

Cashflow

Definition:
Cashflow - The total amount of money being transferred into and out of a business, especially as affecting liquidity.

In other words, cashflow is a virtual move of money from one investment to another.

Cashflow assets require an investment of either time or money. REITs, dividend stocks, real estate, and crowdfunding are easy income generators which involve investing your money. You can invest in single or multi-family real estate if you're willing to take risks.

Cashflow is probably one of the most important words when creating wealth. Money was created to flow just like energy. If your money isn't making money, you're losing money. Save your money to invest and keep an open stream of income pouring in at all times.

The average millionaire has seven sources of income. So with that being said, it's safe to say the name of the game is creating multiple streams of income. The famous rapper 50cent once said you're not making-money until you're making money in your sleep. Creating positive cashflow is always a great way to build wealth and obtain financial freedom.

Taxes

In this chapter I will share with you several positive cashflow producing investments that can put you ahead of the game. There are 1 million ways to make 1 million dollars. Find an investment vehicle of your choice and invest wisely. However, remember how you generate the million dollars will determine the amount of taxes you pay to Uncle Sam, himself. I was once told by a billionaire if you don't understand how taxes work, good luck on becoming rich or even financially free.

Taxes are your single highest debt so it is crucial that you learn how taxes work. Like most billionaires and millionaires say, if you don't understand how to do it, pay someone who does!

Reading my book, you'll learn why the rich pay less in taxes than the poor and how you can position yourself to do the same.

Assets and Liabilities

My four-year-old daughter, "Boss Lady" Mia, can tell you the difference between an asset and a liability. When she's asked, "What does an asset do?" she replies, "Put money in your pocket!" When asked, "What does a liability do?", she replies "Takes money out of your pocket!"

As simple as this may seem, a lot of people tend to complicate it. Understanding how to read a financial statement or balance sheet is very critical when dealing with assets and liabilities. You have to know what's producing income after your expenses are paid.

These are things that aren't taught in our school system. Our school system is structured to create employees, not entrepreneurs. This is one of the reasons 95% of our population is living paycheck to paycheck. Financial literacy is scarce in today's society. Understanding how to manage your money starts with knowing the differences between an asset and liability. In the asset and liability chapter I will break down different methods you can use to build income producing assets and liabilities that I would advise you to stay away from.

Generational Wealth

Generational wealth is passed down throughout generation to generation. American examples include the Rockefellers, the Kennedys, and the Walton families. Some of the rich and famous inherit millions, sometime billions of dollars. But without financial education to multiply this wealth, it's almost impossible to hold or pass it down through generations; unless it is indestructible wealth, or as I call it, “the water well that keeps on giving”.

Whether you have been on the giving end or the receiving end of generational wealth, we all know it is more than a gift, cash for finishing your chores, or a handout. This type of wealth is a display of years of hard work, and the teaching of financial literacy through generations. It carries a piece of your heritage and helps tell your family story. You too can leave a legacy like they have for your own children. I will show you how to create wealth for future generations in this chapter.

Recessions are the Black Fridays for the Rich

Although the 2020 coronavirus was a real tragedy that claimed many lives, I also felt it was a way for the government to cause a recession and alter the flow of income for millions of people. Recessions are the Black Fridays for the rich. Just think about it - this pandemic sent the world into a frenzy. For example, all of the toilet paper was pretty much nonexistent. People literally stocked up on toilet paper, which raised toilet paper demand due to impulsive decision making. While the poor bought toilet paper, the rich were buying stocks.

This all goes back to the mindset the rich strategize and planned, while the poor panic. My question to you is, were you one of those individuals making impulsive decisions based on the event that took place? Were you affected by coronavirus? Did you lose your job or were you forced to close your business? Times like these are where “recession proof” doesn't sound too bad. Not being affected by what's going on in the world is a blessing within itself. I'll share how the rich capitalized from this pandemic.

The rich make the majority of their money in a down market. In other words, when the world is in a financial crisis, that's when the rich become laser focused. Why? Irrational or impulsive decision making by 95% of our population during uncertain times allow the other 5% to profit. It's simple supply and demand effects. For example, during the 2020 Covid-19 pandemic, frantic people began panic buying all available toilet paper, creating a shortage, which increased the demand for the product. This resulted in the manufacturing companies market demand and profit margins increasing drastically. Supply and demand at work!

The Financial Freedom Cashflow Meter

- Employees make their bosses rich.
- Corruption makes politicians rich.
- Debtors make the banks rich.
- Investors make themselves rich.

Therefore, you always have to position yourself to become an investor.

These are 6 Simple Steps How to Get Rich

Step 1: Commit - Becoming rich starts with your mindset, with the belief that you really can accumulate wealth.
Step 2: Assets and Liabilities - Know the difference
Step 3: Increase Your Income and Reduce your Expenses
Step 4: Find a Mentor
Step 5: Live Below Your Means - Stay Broke
Step 6: Save To Invest, Don't Save To Save

The Money Secret

No matter how much money you make, whether it's $30,000 a year; $60,000 a month; $80,000 a day; $200,000 a month; or $500,000 a day; the key to building wealth remains the same:

Make money, use your money to make more money, and live below your means.

There you have it, this is the secret everyone's been looking for with a splash of Mindset, and an understanding how money works (before, during or after a pandemic). The key is positioning yourself in a down and up market. During down times, like during the coronavirus pandemic, the world was in chaos and the supply and demand cycle fluctuated drastically which caused a chain of reactions.

I've studied some of the most successful people and everyone seems to have the same strategy when it comes to building wealth: create multiple streams of income. The more streams of income you have, the better your chances of becoming successful. Visualize it. Plan it. Now apply and execute it.

Here are some of the money pools that created serious income during the pandemic:

1. Stock Market. During this time, the stock market fluctuates aggressively. A bullish market meaning stocks that are rising aggressively. A bear market describes when stocks drop drastically, which is perfect for gaining long-term and short-term profits.
2. Online Sales. People are frantic and begin to make impulsive purchases which then raises demand for products. Online shopping increased due to the fear of being exposed to virus.
3. Real Estate. The crisis caused people to lose their jobs and forced many to fall victim to foreclosure, which is where the rich capitalize by buying properties below market value.
4. Financial Institutions. Leveraged the banks money to invest wisely.
5. Life Insurance – The rich also invested in untouchable life insurance, where their money would multiply itself from compound interest.

Think Like the Rich!

Before you speak - Listen.

Before you spend - Earn.
Before you quit – Try.
Most importantly, before you die - Live.

There are 4 types of Wealth

1. Financial Wealth - MONEY
2. Social Wealth - STATUS
3. Time Wealth - FREEDOM
4. Physical Wealth - HEALTH

Be careful of jobs that lure you into 1 and 2,
But rob you of 3 and 4.

The 21/90 Rule

Have you ever heard of the 21/90 rule? It takes 21 days to build a habit and 90 days to create a lifestyle? You just have to make a conscious decision to become successful and apply what you have learned into your day-to-day life.

There is an important term you should get very familiar with on this journey to Financial freedom: Positive Cashflow. Ask yourself what is your monthly positive cashflow. Multiply that monthly cashflow by 12. Then ask yourself if you were to negate 40% for taxes and 40% for investment storage, would the remaining 20% will fund your lifestyle? Are you making enough to maintain a comfortable lifestyle? If not, I advise you to get back to the drawing board and map out a plan to create some serious passive and residual income.

In other words, create cashflow with multiple streams of income. While you are out spending, the rich are usually out building multiple streams of income to create passive and residual income - making money while they sleep.

Learn how to position yourself and obtain financial freedom by enrolling in my Monal Capital Financial Literacy platform. The Financial Freedom Hacks course, where you will receive mind blowing information guiding you into an abundance of wealth, but only if you apply what you have learned.

Here is some free game on how to put yourself in a position to gain financial freedom. Thank me later!

Free Game - Your Credit Score

Would you rather have an 850 credit score or $100,000 dollars? The majority of rich and successful people started off leveraging good credit. The key to leveraging good credit to generate wealth is to develop good spending habits, live within your means and maintain a good credit score. The higher your credit score, the less you pay for interest on loans, and the easier it will be to establish business relationships.

Building Your Credit to Build Wealth

Repair Credit Problems

1. What is your credit score?
2. Remove any erroneous or obsolete items from your credit reports.
3. Challenge all of those negative items with the credit bureaus to have them removed. I can help you with that:

   Step 1: Basic Dispute. You always start by correcting extra names, addresses, and employment info on your credit report. Then you include inquiries, collection accounts, closed accounts. You'll receive letters back notifying you if the items were removed or verified. Then you proceed to step 2.

   Step 2: The 609 Letter (aka the *Prove It* Letter). The Fair Credit Reporting Act contains 25 sections, numbered 601 through 625. The 609 letter is based on rights granted under Section 609 of the Fair Credit Reporting Act. Under Section 609, credit reporting agencies are required to disclose certain information to consumers who request it. Specifically, consumers are allowed to request (1) All the information on your credit report, and (2) the source of the information on your credit report.

   Step 3: Validation of Debt Letter to Creditor. Immediately after you receive your credit bureau results (from the 609 letter), whichever delinquent accounts were included, put them in the Validation of Debt letter and send it to each creditor (NOT the credit bureaus).

If you see there are issues due to identity theft, file a FTC Identity Theft Affidavit. You'll need to file a police report and say you lost your wallet, purse, etc. a few years ago (before your negative accounts were opened). Then you'll need to get it notarized, and add it to a package, along with an Identity Theft Dispute letter, 502 law, a copy of your ID, a copy of your utility bill and send it to the Consumer Finance Protection Bureau (CFPB). CFPB is the government regulator over the credit bureaus. To remove negative items, you can also use CFPB.gov. It is more time consuming, but very effective.

Build Your Credit

1. Now it's time to build your credit! First, you can add a positive tradeline to your credit history. Become an authorized user on someone else's good credit card history.
2. Apply for revolving credit, such as a personal loan, car payment, mortgage, credit cards, etc. This builds you credit history.
3. Make sure you're making your payments on time.
4. Now leverage or even liquidate your credits to purchase investments.

Purchase my Financial Freedom Hacks to get more step-by-step help on how to remove negative items and how to build your credit at www.financialfreedomhacks.org.

Free Game – Build a E-Commerce Business

Jeff Bezos makes $13 million in one hour. His company, Amazon, is on the verge of becoming the world's second trillion-dollar company, behind Apple. Success leaves clues - become a seller, not a buyer with an E-commerce business.

How to Build an E-Commerce Business:

1. Create a Multi-service Limited Liability Company (LLC)
2. Apply for an IRS Employer Identification Number (EIN)
3. Apply for a state reseller certificate, which is a document that allows retailers to purchase goods for resale without having to pay local sales tax for those items.
4. Start an Amazon seller account.
5. Make sure you have a line of credit available.
6. Use social media platform for paid ads to monetize your products.
7. Sell those Products on the Amazon platform.
8. Scale your store up to $100,000 in sales a month.

I've done it. It can be so simple, but we as people tend to complicate things. The rich find solutions, the poor find excuses.

Purchase my Financial Freedom Hacks to get more step-by-step instructions on how to build a successful ecommerce business at www.financialfreedomhacks.org.

Free Game – Real Estate Investing

Over the last two centuries, about 90 % of the world's millionaires have been created by investing in real estate. For the average investor, real estate offers the best way to develop significant wealth. Real estate investing offers great tax benefits, such as writing off depreciation, mortgage interest, repair costs, etc., etc. Over time appreciation and growth builds equity throughout the years. But most importantly, real estate investment can also generate cashflow through passive income.

Here are a few real estate investing methods:

1. Wholesaling:

a. Find an absentee owners' property.
b. Put the property under contract with an assignment clause. An assignment clause allows you, the wholesaler, to assign the contract to a third-party seller.
c. Wholesale the property. Use the assignment clause to match a buyer and seller. The seller agrees to sell and buyer agrees to buy the property and you, the wholesaler, facilitates the deal without actually owning the property, and without the need for cash to close the deal.

2. Invest in multi-unit properties, like duplexes, or multi-family buildings to create a monthly cashflow.
3. Purchase rehab properties. Invest into renovation properties, then resell them for profit.
4. Next level goals: Purchase apartment buildings to create residual monthly income. (Generational wealth)

Purchase my Financial Freedom Hacks to get more step-by-step instructions on how to create passive and residual income in real estate at www.financialfreedomhacks.org.

CHAPTER 1

Mindset

MINDSET

I changed my mindset and it changed my life!
Do what the 99% percent are not doing!

Starting this chapter off with questions:
What does it mean to have financial freedom?

Becoming financially free isn't something everyone wants for themselves, although I think it's something that everyone should experience.

Are you Listening to the Right People? Who do you spend the majority of your time with? Where are these people at in life? Are they employees, business owners or investors?

I ask you this question because the people you spend the majority of your time with can be the results of your future. Show me your friends and I'll show you, your future!

If you could start all over again, what would you do differently? Would you have changed your mindset? When someone says to you that they're going to be rich and successful, what are the first thoughts that come to mind? Then and Now.

Are they positive thoughts? (you agree)
Or are they negative thoughts? (doubtful)

Your mental approaches to life situations are key to your journey to success.

If you learn how to think correctly financial freedom is obtainable. I want to teach you how to think correctly. The largest gap between successful and unsuccessful people is the mentality gap. I'm not talking about being smart or having a high IQ. I'm talking about how you think and process information. Successful people think differently than unsuccessful people. If you want to have a fulfilled life you must fill your mind correctly.

> **"There are no limits to what you can accomplish except the limits you place on your own thinking."**
>
> \- Brian Tracy

> **"It's going to be hard, but hard does not mean impossible."**
>
> \- Anonymous

Positive thinking is a mental and emotional attitude that focuses on the bright side of life and expects positive results. Approach life's challenges with a positive outlook. It does not necessarily mean avoiding or ignoring the bad things; instead, it involves making the most of the potentially bad situations, trying to see the best in other people and viewing yourself and your abilities in a positive light. If your outlook on success is negative, how can you envision someone's goals of becoming successful, when you yourself can't envision yourself being successful?

Once you say no to an opportunity or have a negative outlook on an opportunity your brain shuts down, and is no longer interested.
It's so easy to say you can't do something versus finding a way to do it!

The mind is the most powerful thing that we possess. What you feed your mind is what it creates. The person making $ 5 million per year believes their going make that. It's all they can see. They know they're capable of doing so. The person making $50k per year believes that maybe $100k per year is the goal but is just limited by their own beliefs. Break all limitations!

Be open minded to the information that you're about to receive and allow yourself a chance to process valuable information.

Learn to Think Big

You must learn to think BIG. Break down the barriers in your mind! You cannot achieve, build, nor accomplish anything that your mind can't conceive. Most individuals think being rich is based on how much money you have. But in all actuality, being rich is nothing more than a mindset! People must understand that your mind must arrive to the designation before your life does.

Your WHY has to be strong ENOUGH
Your why will give you the motivation to do anything you set your mind to.

How to identify your why!

Why do you want change?
Why do you want to start your business?
why do you want to take your income to the next Level?
Why do you want to have Joy and happiness daily?
Once you have identified your why, the mind begins to manifest everything into reality. Your why should be your motivation.

My why has always been happiness, but once my daughter came into this world, she became my why. Happiness and Mia Amora are now my whys!

Your approach to life!

Sacrifice today so you won't have to compromise in the future. The way you approach obstacles that are place in your life is what defines you as an individual.

You must train your mind to find solutions instead of excuses (Think like the rich).

Are You Aligned with the right people?

Stop Poverty Behavior

Growing up in poverty, I was brought up to think in a systematic way, following guidelines created to alter the way of thinking. Your environment can have a negative or positive impact on your life but it's all about perception.

Having a certain mindset can be contagious that's why it's very important for you to surround yourself with like-minded and goal-oriented people. People who can help you elevate your life and your way of thinking.

Negative Nancy people can be very detrimental to your life and your way of thinking. For example, a shark in a fish tank will grow 8 inches, but in the ocean, it will grow to 8 feet or more. The shark will never outgrow its environment and the same is true about you. Many times, we're around small thinking people so we don't grow. Change your environment and watch your growth.

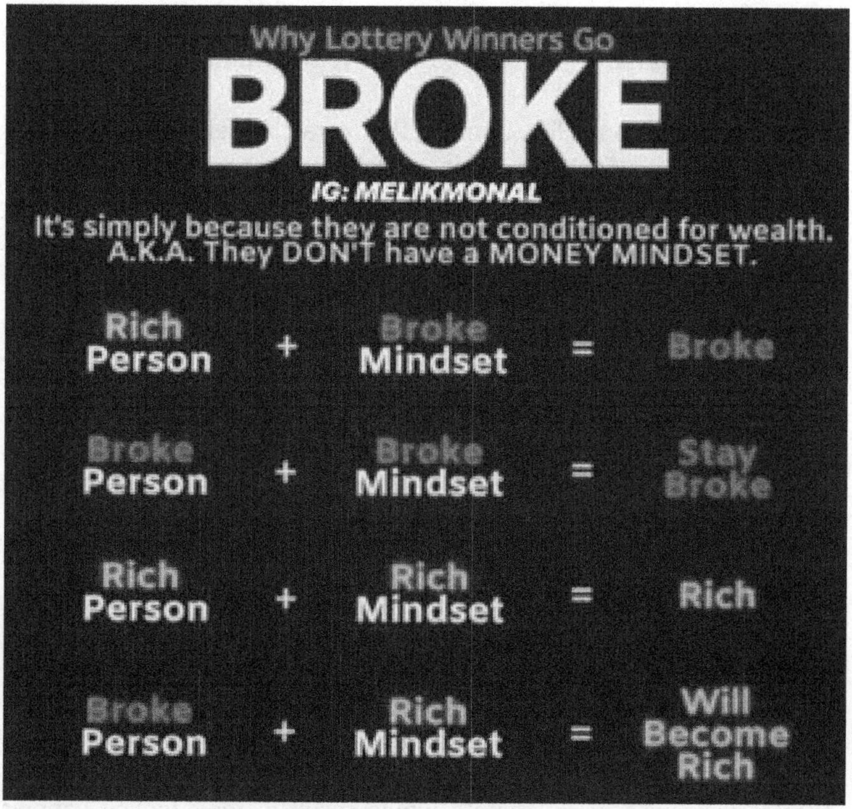

Becoming Successful Starts with You

Success in the dictionary is defined as "the accomplishment of an aim or purpose." Most people think of money and possessions as markers or indicators of success.

As human beings, Abraham Maslow's hierarchy of needs proposes that we have five distinct needs that need to be satisfied, in the following order:

1. Basic needs: water, air, food and shelter
2. Safety: e.g., protection from physical harm, financial security to support our needs
3. Social needs: human requirement for companionship

4. Esteem needs – the desire for respect, or, to flaunt wealth/prestige
5. Self-actualization – the need to reach your full potential

Many of us go through life, climbing this hierarchy, seldom reaching the top. Our lives comprise of a great struggle to reach self-actualization or what can also be referred to as "success."

What's very entertaining is finding out who you truly are when you have nothing.

A study of wealthy Americans revealed that 37% were less happy than the average American. So, if the pursuit of wealth had resulted in their being unhappy, that would make them "successfully unsuccessful." Research also shows that some people do not understand the difference between what they think (or feel) will make them happy and what will genuinely bring about happiness.

This begs the question, "What then is genuine success, and how can we achieve it?"

Martin Seligman, in his book, *Authentic Happiness*, writes about people in Nebraska wishing that they could live in California because they felt that residing in a warm climate would result in their feeling happier (Seligman, 2017). Intriguingly, research shows that there was no difference in their emotional state because the same causes of stress were present in both the warm and cold locations!

The same can be said of success. You can be successful wherever you are located, if only you deal with the causes of your seeming unsuccessfulness and the resultant dissatisfaction.

What is Genuine Success?

A major flaw with most motivational coaching that encourages cultivating a "successful lifestyle" is that while it helps one set and achieve goals, rarely does it have an enduring positive effect.

How can a human being be referred to as "successful" if in their pursuit of a goal they are miserable, and the satisfaction gained by their attaining their goals is short-lived? To be genuinely successful, one is required to find peace and contentment in current achievements, even while endeavoring towards future goals. Only put your time and effort into what will give you long-lasting joy.

Avoid Regret

Researcher Richard Leider interviewed senior citizens for 25 years, to find out their regrets. From their responses, he compiled the following advice:

- Get out of the rat race. Take time to work out what you want from life
- Be courageous, take risks, be adventurous. You come alive when stretching, exploring and growing
- Time is your most valuable currency. Find out, as early as possible, what fulfills and satisfies you internally. Success is not about the size of your house, your titles, or accolades but what makes you emotionally whole and at peace

Seligman a proponent of "positive psychology," proposed that people can improve their lives and make them more productive, and fulfilled by:

- Setting the desired and proper goals (what do you really want to achieve, that will truly satisfy you?)
- Meeting those goals while enjoying the process (how can I purpose to enjoy the process?)

This doesn't mean that life is a bed of roses. Most goals require a certain amount of discomfort, focus, and dedication, e.g., sporting and weight loss.

Setting Life Goals

When setting life goals, Psychologist Dr. Alison Price recommends using the FLOURISH model. The question in mind, while considering your life goals should be, "How will achieving these goals help me **FLOURISH** in the following areas of my life?"

F: **Friends** – those that you trust and who you socialize with
L: **Love** – romantic relationships (spouses)
O: **Occupation** – your career, how you spend your 'work' time
U: **Usual environment** – home, it's setting, the lifestyle opportunities it provides
R: **Relatives** – relationships with family members
I: **Income** – your finances
S: **Spare time** – your 'free' time, how you spend it
H: **Health** – your physical wellbeing

With that said, let's begin with the end in mind.

First, set goals that make your relationships as secure as possible. No man is an island; having social relationships and friends you can trust makes us feel happy and fulfilled.

Second, set meaningful goals. Granted, most of us stumble through life not knowing who we are and what we want, other than to meet our basic needs. Setting goals requires a lot of self-examination, even interviewing friends and family to find out what your strengths are. It is best to find out what these are and align yourself to them as soon as is possible, even while drafting brand new life goals.

Fulfillment can only be achieved when you live your life with a sense of meaning and purpose. A fitting question to ask is, "If money was not an object, what would you spend time doing?"

Third, adversity can refine your character and help you become a better person. American social psychologist Dr. Haidt learned that tremendous struggle could make human beings grow and cause them to prioritize better. Adversity, when viewed as a help rather than a hindrance, can help one filter out time-wasting negativity and pettiness. How you respond to life events is critical to your future wellbeing.

Respond to hardships wisely and with a calm and retrospective mind, and you will prevail.

Fourth, carpe diem! Seize the day! Make the most of every opportunity to better yourself. Don't wait for a wakeup call to stir you to action. Change your life now, while you still live, dream, and hope for the future. Time is very precious, make the most of your days doing what satisfies and rewards you the most.

Principles of Success

Perhaps the most renown author on success is Napoleon Hill. In his books *Keys to Success* and *Think and Grow Rich*, he lists 17 principles of success that are applicable today as they were 80 years ago (Hill and Sartwell, 2017; Hill and Cornwell, 2019).

1. **Definiteness of Purpose**
   All achievement has a definite beginning. Your quest to succeed in life, be it in your career or personal life, starts with you (first) having a purpose.

2. **Mastermind Alliance**
   Work in harmony with like-minded people to achieve goals. Select your partners carefully and work in tandem to obtain a common objective. Working in partnership with skilled individuals helps your team achieve its goals much faster.

3. **Applied Faith**
   Use the power of faith to achieve your goals. Faith is the extra ingredient that allows you to tap into the unseen realm, opening infinite possibilities.

4. **Go the Extra Mile**
   Quality of service + quantity of service + positive mental attitude= compensation. The more the effort applied, the more the reward.

This law applies to every facet of life, i.e., money, joy, relationships, etc.

5. **Attractive Personality**
   Working with a pleasant personality makes goals that much simpler to achieve. According to Hill, you can transform 25 characteristics of your personality to become a better version of you.

6. **Personal Initiative**
   To achieve greatness, go the extra mile. Be a self-starter who does not need supervision.

7. **Positive Mental Attitude**
   Maintain a positive attitude, even when facing adversity. Power through challenges with a clear and focused mind.

8. **Enthusiasm**
   Enthusiasm is an external expression of faith, hope, and belief. It radiates from within your soul, brightening your countenance while inspiring and energizing the team that you work with.

9. **Self-discipline**
   Master your thoughts and needs to be able to achieve your goals. You become a slave to whatever you cannot control, e.g., ambition, anger, etc.

10. **Accurate Thinking**
    Guard your mind, encourage clean, and clear thoughts. Focus on what is useful and essential, eliminate idle thoughts from your mind. You become what you think.

11. **Controlled Attention**
    Maintain your focus on what will enable you to achieve your goals. Prioritize your mind, time, energy and resources to achieving goals.

12. **Teamwork**
    Working together enables a team to accomplish much and faster.

13. **Adversity and Defeat**
    Grow from your mistakes and learn from them. Human is to error.

14. **Creative Vision**
    Use your imagination, nurture your powers of creativity to overcome obstacles and provide revolutionary and pioneering solutions.

15. **Health**
    Manage your health by eating healthily, exercising, reading, and challenging your mind. A healthy mind, body, and spirit enjoys life and its successes.

16. **Budgeting Time and Money**
    Be wise in how you allocate your time, money, and other resources. Align your expenditure on achieving goals. Waste not, want not.

17. **Habits**
    Develop good habits to achieve peace of mind, financial security, and good health. Thoughts lead to deeds, and deeds become habits. Live wisely.

Rich Mindset vs Poor Mindset

The number one rule in building a wealthy mindset is: Don't be a slave to money! (Exchanging time for money). The rich don't work for money. Working for money only guarantees one thing and that's taxes (Uncle Sam).

The rich open businesses and invest in real estate so that money works for them. And they usually pay no taxes (residual income).

It's not just about money. You must step back and look at the bigger picture. Once you take a paycheck, you become an employee... and that's the mindset you keep. Receiving a paycheck isn't the problem. The problem is, the mindset you now have because you're being given something versus you creating it yourself.

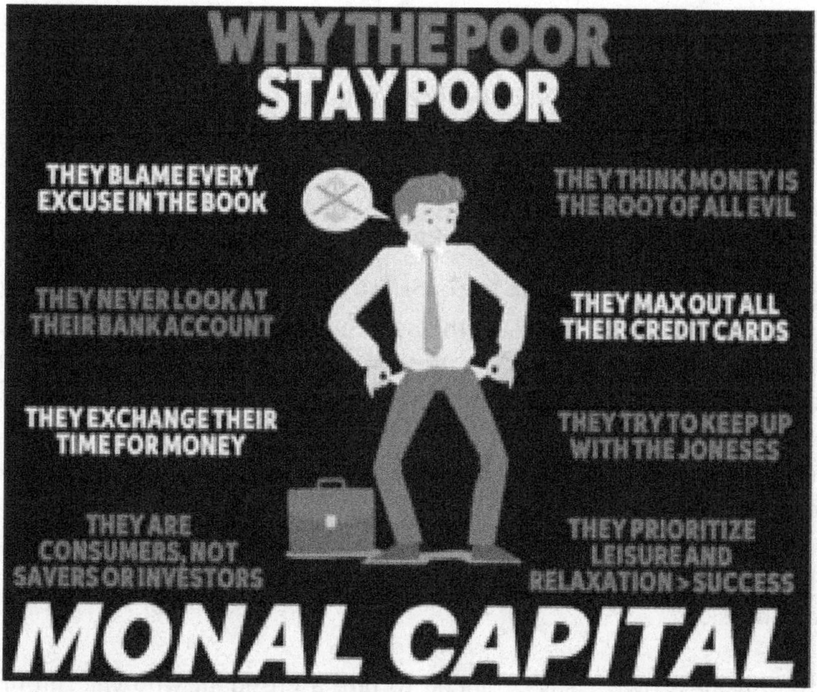

Become an Entrepreneur

An entrepreneur's first job is to control what's going on internally before taking on the world itself. Entrepreneurship is a mindset first, skillset second, understanding rules last. And within that journey, there's something called failure.

There's no success without failure. It is at this point as an Entrepreneur, when you don't have a consistent paycheck, you become hungrier, and smarter.

Every success and failure are a test of your character.
Will you become a crook?
Will you become greedy?
Will you cheat and steal?
Or will you become a better human being?
When facing challenges in adversity as an entrepreneur!

One thing about becoming an entrepreneur you really find out who you are when you don't have anything. But nowadays as an entrepreneur you have more control over your finances. You control how much money you make and how much you pay back in taxes (income control).

Four Classifications of People

Robert Kiyosaki, in his book *The CASHFLOW Quadrant®*, classifies people into four groups: employees, the self-employed, business owners and investors. "Listen to a person's words and actions," he says, "and you'll have a window into which mindset they hold" (Kiyosaki, 2011).

The employee says: "I'm looking for a job with good pay and excellent benefits."

The self-employed says: "My rate is $35 an hour" or "I charge a 6 percent commission."

The business owner says: "I need to hire a President who will run my company."

The investor says: "My team will study the valuation of that company."

There is no wrong group. There's just a lifestyle that fits your criteria at that time in your life.

Be Content

Be aware that when you achieve your goals, research shows that people adapt to their successes and yearn to achieve bigger and flashier goals. This cycle is referred to by psychologists as hedonic adaptation.

For example, when you drive your sports car for the first time, you feel excited — the second time, less enthusiastic. By the 547th time, you will not have any reaction to being in that sports car. Matter of fact, you'll be desiring a new car.

Ultimately, enjoy your life, practice contentment, and choose a path that you'll have fun traveling on as you pursue success. Be sure to apply all these principles to achieve success in your life!

Being Wealthy is a Mindset

The most efficient way to increase your chances of becoming wealthy is to change your mindset. One's state of mind determines the daily effort that will be applied towards achieving goals. So, before you can accomplish that lofty goal, you must believe that you can do so. We tend to underestimate the mental power required to achieve even the smallest of goals, leading to a cycle of struggle and sense of defeat.

I've got wonderful news for you- it does not have to be that way! All you need to do is rewire your thinking, and this can be done sooner than you think with little effort and some determination.

Starting now, move from thinking about earning a basic income and find ways to generate wealth.

A Wealth Mindset - What is it?

Mindset is defined as: An inclination or state of mind. A mental attitude.

Therefore, a wealth mindset means a mental attitude that enables us to focus on prosperity, increase, and abundance.

Surprisingly, people focus on the direct opposite when longing to become wealthy. They concentrate on desiring prosperity and needing wealth and wanting to pursue both. To be clear, the emphasis is on wishful thinking; on mulling over the fact that they are neither prosperous nor wealthy, indicating a poverty or scarcity mindset.

Thoughts and words such as "I wish I had that Ferrari" or "If only I had a mansion with an infinity pool" come to mind. Their attention is on what they lack – what they do not have.

Don't worry; it is very natural to have this mindset! However, moving forward, you will need to be willing to transform your thinking and have the courage to act upon your new attitude by strictly focusing on the pursuit of wealth.

Abundance Versus Scarcity

Begin by expanding your perception of wealth. Perhaps you are currently in the habit of looking at the negative side of every situation. Perhaps the pressure of unpaid bills is steadily mounting; too much month with too little money remaining.

To turn this negative perception around, practice observing abundance around you:

- Be grateful for the resources and money that you currently have. Name the resources, and the amount of money; meditate on the sense of thankfulness rising in your heart and mind. Thank God audibly for the money and resources
- Embrace a sense of optimism; you will earn more soon
- Believe that you are on the path to making more money - to changing your life

Reflections on Wealth

You attract what you are and believe. If you look down upon wealthy people and sneer at wealth, it'll be tough to become wealthy. For the simple reason that every time you speak or think about wealth, your negativity will block you from attracting wealth.

To counter this habit, look for wealthy people that you can admire without too much effort. Immerse yourself in captivating articles and books about celebrities and philanthropists who donate their money towards worthy causes. Seek out rags-to-riches stories about self-made millionaires.

As you focus on the good that can be achieved by being wealthy, your perception will begin to change, causing you to draw tangible expressions of prosperity and wealth into your life.

Avoid Negativity

While deliberately focusing on wealth and success, in the same measure, start to ignore and avoid examples of scarcity – both in the world and in your life.

Switch off the news, don't gaze woefully at derelict buildings or any symbol of poverty. This habit of pondering over negativity, unfortunately, becomes part and parcel of our lives, causing us to obsess about the challenges and problems in our personal lives.

Why should we linger over disappointments and challenges? It causes us to become fixated on problems, which in turn makes us feel out of control, even helpless.

Therefore, train your mind to turn away from distractions that prevent you from focusing on your well-being and becoming wealthy. This does not mean that you develop an alternate reality where you escape responsibilities, e.g., overdue bills. Purpose to focus on the good and not the negative.

A good rule of thumb is: Improve the situation at hand and then immediately move on to more wealth enhancing pursuits. Do not wallow in failure. Avoid fretting over bills and lack of funds. Encourage yourself to take decisive action towards resolving your financial situation.

Be precise and proactive in your efforts, all the while focusing on where you want to go and not where you currently are and don't want to be.

For example, if on a road trip, you were to drive while only looking into your rearview mirror, you would very likely crash.

Perception: Be Proactive

Your perception of life's circumstances is critical. Why? Because many of us spend our lives reacting to circumstances — that is, we only act after something has happened.

For example, if we perceive danger, we act in defense of ourselves. If we think of ourselves as lacking in opportunities and or poor, we may give in to despair and stop looking for solutions to improve the situation. These reactions, in turn, become self-fulfilling prophecies.

An overly defensive person can provoke attacks, while an excessively pessimistic one can attract more issues, preventing them from improving their lives.

Let go of the reactive mindset and embrace a proactive mindset instead.

Remove Limitations

Do you have perceived limits about becoming successful and wealthy?

- Are you aware that you can earn a better income?
- Do you think that an absence of opportunities prevents you from earning more money?
- Do you feel that there are numerous obstacles in your path making your journey to prosperity that much harder?

Document every limitation that comes to mind that you feel hinders you from attaining wealth. Include inner (internal emotional responses) and outer (external factors e.g., environmental, situational) limits. List your doubts and fears, as well as any other perceived challenges, e.g., lack of opportunities.

Read each entry carefully, questioning the veracity of each statement – decide if it's true or false. You'll be surprised to find that you have believed lies.

For example, the statement, “I cannot earn more money because I did not graduate from college,” there is a list of millionaires and billionaires who never attended college or who dropped out of college, or even high school. This eye-opening process will help you see the limitations you’ve placed upon yourself.

Constantly challenge these false perceptions in order to uproot them from your subconscious mind. Act against your limiting thoughts and experience victory!

Develop a Millionaires Mindset

Plan to get wealthy slowly but surely. Avoid “get rich quick” schemes and do not lose money.

Dedicate substantial amounts of time studying investment opportunities. The average person spends 2-3 hours monthly thinking about money, usually when the bills are due. By contrast, a self-made millionaire spends 20-30 hours per month planning their investment strategy. Substantial financial planning invariably leads to wise decisions and excellent results.

Cultivate Millionaire Habits

Self-made millionaires develop an array of financial habits in their quest for prosperity, they:

- Seek out, competent financial advisors. Excellent advisors can be the difference between making a lot of money or losing it.
- Investigate before investing in any business deals. Find out as much information about a potential deal/investment.
- Don't rush their decision making. Millionaires take their time in making decisions.
- Reject business deals. Learn to walk away from deals that look too good to be true.
- Do not take unnecessary chances or gamble. They make conscientious decisions based on reliable information, while continually asking, "What's the worst-case scenario?"

- Protect their assets with excellent legal representation and insurance. Just in case you get sued, ensure that your business is an LLC (Limited Liability Company), at a minimum, and has proper registration, licensing and insurance.
- Spend wisely and negotiate effectively. Be prudent about how you spend money. Always go for the best quality at the lowest price. Monitor every dollar you spend.

Act

With the sure and steady transformation of your mind, you are now able to take focused action. So, what should that action be?

One thing that the world's wealthiest and most successful people have in common is that they contribute value and are wonderfully rewarded.

Reflect on that.

Becoming wealthy is not about wishful thinking or escapism. If that ever works for you, please tell me! Most successful people have had to work hard for their wealth. Thankfully, most of them also enjoy what they do. Leading to another point: your wealth potential is tucked among your passions and interests. Being passionate is not enough. Your desires should be able to fabulously compensate you. What do you love to do? Utilize your talents and interests to contribute value.

How? Some examples Include:

- Write and sell an e-book, on a topic of interest, e.g., sci-fi.
- Create a product, e.g., design clothes, create an app.
- Offer a service, e.g., Emceeing at weddings, start a cleaning company.

The possibilities are endless. Consider your skills and what you genuinely enjoy doing and ask yourself, "How can I use these assets to generate income while also contributing value?"

Change the Way You Work

To obtain wealth, approach the activities that you have in mind with a can-do attitude. The wrong way is to take small actions while hoping for tremendous results, and declaring defeat if progress isn't as expected. The above approaches are as different as day and night - one path guarantees success, while the other leads to failure.

Try this instead:

- Take courageous and consistent actions daily.

- Do hard tasks first when you have the energy and focus.
- Venture away from your comfort zone.
- Be confident about your skills and abilities. Expect good results.
- Be patient – there's no such thing as overnight success.
- Enjoy the journey to success.

Do not focus on results, relax, do your best, and the rest will happen naturally. A relaxed attitude helps you progress faster, compared to complaining and getting frustrated.

Practice Contentment

A common misconception is that achieving monetary success will bring about happiness. While having money does alleviate stress and allows you to enjoy financial freedom, becoming wealthy does not guarantee satisfaction.

On any given day, the tabloids are jam-packed with stories about sad wealthy people who have one type of crisis after another, from divorces to drug addictions. Having bucket loads of money does not inoculate you from life's circumstances that cannot be resolved with money.

So, practice contentment. An increase in money will simply help you feel even more fulfilled! Change your mindset. Be confident and become a problem solver.

Now the question is...are you going to apply what you have read to your day-to-day life? Reading this book won't make you a millionaire, but applying what you have read in this book might! Most people don't take action. Don't be like most people. Apply the information in these pages to your life.

Surrounding yourself with millionaires won't make you a millionaire, but applying what you've learned from millionaires will!

Don't cheat yourself out of an opportunity. You can plan goal setting with a pencil, but you have to do goal getting with your legs! You have to take action!!

The biggest gap in this world is the act of knowing and doing knowing is goal setting and doing is goal achieving!!

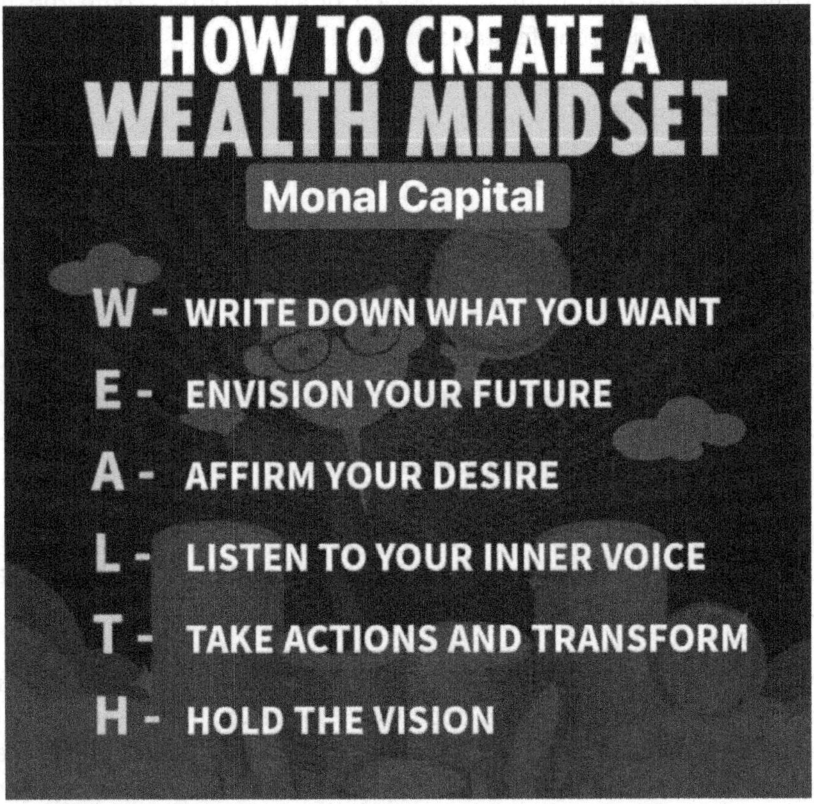

CHAPTER 2

Credit and Debt

CREDIT AND DEBT

Cash Is King, But Credit Is Power

Credit is defined as the ability of a customer to obtain goods or services before payment, based on the trust that payment will be made in the future.

The rich leverage other people's money (OPM) to make more money. Financial institutions (banks) Are a great a way to leverage your buying power using their line of credit to purchase assets, the rich leverage the banks money to pour into income producing investments. Did you know an 800-credit score has a "buying power" of $300,000? Imagine Receiving $300,000 to invest into any investment vehicle of your choice? Powerful, right? That's what the rich do – leverage.

Good Debt And Bad Debt

Good debt is always considered debt that is used to buy assets. For example, if you were to use $100,000 to purchase a passive income producing property. The rich used debt to become richer.

Facts: In 1971 President Nixon took the dollar off the gold standard and money became debt.

Bad debt is always considered debt that is used to buy liabilities. For example, if you were to use your credit card to buy $10,000 floor seats ticket at a Lakers game. I'm a huge Lakers fan, but buying floor seats doesn't put money in my pocket.

Leveraging Your Credit

Debt is a necessary part of life. While no one likes making interest payments, saving for major purchases, e.g., a house – is not always possible. Interestingly, purchasing a home outrightly is sometimes not the smartest thing to do financially.

Therefore, because the likelihood of having to take on debt is high, how can you ensure that it's worth it? How do you establish that the interest rate offered is worth the benefit of taking on debt? Good debt builds your financial future, while bad debt destroys it. Thankfully, what you are buying can make that distinction clear.

But first, let's talk about the role your credit score plays when taking on debt.

Debt and Credit Scores

One way to generate wealth, through leveraging credit, is by having a good credit score of 700 and above. The importance of having good credit is in the savings you'll make on loan repayments. Even one percentage point saves you $20 - $300 per month. You can then put your savings to good use by investing or borrowing money to purchase wealth-generating assets.

A credit score of 700 and above can help you in the following ways by:

- Increasing your financing options
- Getting low-interest rates
- Enabling you to pay less for purchases
- Spurring competition between financial institutions and companies for your business
- Granting you opportunities to invest in profitable ventures
- Having a solid and respectable credit rating
- Getting approval for higher credit limits and larger loans
- Providing faster approval times
- Giving a favorable impression of you when applying for employment

With a good credit rating, leveraging your credit to generate wealth becomes that much easier. If you have a credit score of less than 700, work on rebuilding it for a more pleasant process when seeking financing.

Secret: When money is being printed, the rich that leverage debt become richer, but the people who are saving are losing money. The banks are charging you interest for money your savings. Debt and taxes make the rich richer and the middle class and poor, poorer.

What Is Good Debt?

When people say get out of debt what is the first thing that comes to mind?

Debt is very powerful and can be used to generate income!

Although debt is considered bad, there are instances when acquiring debt pays future dividends. If you're knowledgeable with leveraging debt like the rich.

Mastering Debt

a. **Student Loans:** Student loans increase your earning potential significantly. Compared to those without post-high-school education, a bachelors' degree holder earns 66% more on average, in their lifetime.

b. **Mortgages:** Mortgages are generally considered good debt - after all, you need to live somewhere. So, instead of paying a landlord rent, you build equity with your living expenses. Purchasing a home, which is a real asset if it pouring funds into your pocket.

   More importantly, consider taking a mortgage to purchase an investment property, for example, a rental apartment. Rental units provide cash inflow that can pay off a mortgage, while also allowing for more investment opportunities to become possible. Owning rental property with low overheads and good cash inflow is a critical step in the wealth-building process.

c. **Starting a Business:** What is your passion? How can you convert it into a business opportunity? Research on how to run a business and get started with a small entrepreneurial venture. Home-based businesses in several states have numerous tax write-offs.

   Small business loans help you with startup costs and business expansion. Loans such as the Small Business Association (SBA) loans require comprehensive business plans. Good debt may also be about long-term arbitrage. The stock markets long-term returns historically outpace today's low mortgage interest rates. So, sometimes it's better to leave your money invested, even if you can purchase a home with cash.

d. **Venture Capitalist Firms and Angel Investors:** These are alternative avenues that you can use to obtain capital. With a venture capitalist, you will exchange your company's equity in return for money to grow your business. Venture capital firms expect high returns of 20% or more from the companies they invest in; that is one disadvantage of working with VC's. They also expect quick returns on their investments and tend to exercise a lot of control over a company.

   The advantage of raising funds with a venture capitalist is that most can finance a company, even a startup, with $500,000 to millions of dollars!

   Angel investors are usually affluent individuals who provide business capital in exchange for convertible debt or ownership equity. It's like watching an episode of Shark Tank, with the likes of Mark Cuban buying ownership equity in businesses.

Mortgages, small business loans, student loans, are the most preferred forms of good debt. With that said, even with an excellent credit score, good debt still has risks.

Risks of Good Debt

There are no guarantees when you take on debt, even good debt. Taking on debt is like gambling because one assumes that the future will be favorable. The reality is a college degree does not guarantee you a good salary on graduating; a high mortgage can make saving difficult, and a startup can fail.

Always consider expected returns before taking on good debt. How do you expect your life to change when you take on debt? What can go wrong?

For example, can you afford your mortgage payments on your current salary? What if you lost your job?

40 million households in the United States are referred to as "house poor" because they own a home that they cannot easily afford. High property tax payments and high mortgages make it difficult to save for emergencies, invest for the future, or, cover other expenses.

Make sure that your good debt is manageable – that you can afford it. Just because it is good debt, doesn't mean you should take too much of it – too much of a good thing is bad. Think through repayments carefully, and have a contingency plan in case of surprises, e.g., getting fired, slow business season, etc.

Avoid Bad Debt

Bad debt is debt that won't obtain assets or wealth. Bad debt takes away money from your future to spend today, for frivolous lifestyle reasons.

Other examples of bad debt include:

a. **Payday Loans:** The most prominent example of bad debt, payday loans, are some of the most expensive debt in the United States.

For example, loans under $500, which are due on payday, have fees ranging from $10 - $30 for every $100 borrowed. This can translate to an annual percentage rate of around 400%, for a typical two-week loan.

For this reason, some states prohibit or regulate these loans.

b. **Credit Cards:** With 12% - $30 annual percentage rates, credit card debt for nonessential purchases is bad debt. With a 22% APR credit card, it would take four years to pay off a $500 debt and around $280 in interest.

c. **Auto Loans**: A car depreciates as soon as you drive it off the car lot. It doesn't make sense to pay interest on an asset that continually falls in value. It is wiser to purchase a well-maintained used car.

Don't follow your desire to have a particular lifestyle - for instant gratification. Avoid incurring high-interest debt, or debt on entertainment and consumer goods.

Choose the Right Debt

Protect your future self by being conscious of the purpose and type of debt you're taking on. Good debt can increase your ability to build wealth, afford the things you need, and save. My favorite type of debt, after mortgage for rental properties, is business debt. Depending on the venture, business debt can make all the difference by facilitating the conversion of ideas, hard work, and creativity into billions of dollars.

Good debt has been at the foundation of just about every Fortune 500 company.

Secrets: The more debt you use the less you pay in taxes.

Credit for Business

It is vital for a company to build business credit because it minimizes personal risk exposure – you also don't want a significant drop in your personal credit rating. Also, if your business tanks, there goes your personal credit with it. It is also considered more professional to have business credit. Vendors and new clients run searches to verify if a company has a business credit score. Looking up business scores, unlike personal scores, does not need authorization – anyone can look up your business credit scores.

A startup may be able to support growth with personal loans or credit cards at the beginning. However, that is simply not sustainable. A business loan will be needed to maintain a growing organization. Unfortunately, a new business might not qualify for traditional financing, e.g., SBA loans, short-term loans, business term loans, etc.

There are currently several business loan options for those with zero business credit – options that'll enable one to build credit history in order to qualify for more substantial loans in the future. Many people believe that it's impossible to secure a business loan without business credit. Yes, it can be notoriously difficult, but fortunately for small business owners, not impossible.

Don't worry. There are ways to get cash for your business, by leveraging your personal credit to obtain capital, while building business credit.

Business Credit Card

Business credit cards use an applicant's FICO score to obtain approval. They are excellent for startups because they increase working capital, provide quick access to cash, and have reward incentives while building business credit. A business credit card is flexible enough to cover just about any need that a small business may have.

In addition to working capital, business credit cards can also help in building a business's credit score. Your business credit will be built at a much quicker pace if you put some business expenses on a card, while paying it off with money that you have.

Business Line of Credit

One of the most flexible ways of financing your business is by having a business line of credit. The funds are available when you need it, but you are not under any obligation to use it. Therefore, you will pay interest only on the money used, and not the full amount.

A business credit card and business line have many similarities. However, it is better to choose a business line of credit for the following reasons:

- **When needing cash:** With a line of credit, you can get cash advances of 100% of the permitted amount that you are to able borrow
- **When needing a higher credit limit:** A line of credit offers much higher limits than a credit card
- **When quick repayment isn't possible:** Business lines of credit have a gradual repayment process. So, if you cannot repay in full every month, a line of credit is more advisable, compared to a credit card

To cap it all off, qualifying for a business line of credit is not complicated, with requirements being; a business must be operational for six months before applying and have annual revenue of $50,000.

MONAL CAPITAL

THERE ARE 4 TYPES OF CREDIT

REVOLVING CREDIT

You are given a maximum credit limit, and you can make charges up to that limit. Most credit cards are.

SERVICE CREDIT

Your agreements with service providers are all credit arrangements. You receive electricity, cellular phone service, gym membership, etc.

CHARGE CARDS CREDIT

While they often look like revolving credit cards and are used in the same way, charge accounts differ in that you must pay the total balance every month.

INSTALLMENT CREDIT

You agree to repay the money and interest in regular installments of a fixed amount over a set period of time. Car loans and mortgages are two examples of installment credit.

Accounts Receivable Financing

Turn your IOUs into hard and cold cash. Selling your receivables or purchase orders gives you immediate access to cash, making accounts receivable financing ideal for startups. One's credit rating is irrelevant, to an extent.

Factoring companies take into consideration the credit history of the company that owes you money. That's because that is what determines the likelihood of the factoring company getting paid, as soon as they become owners of the invoice. Accounts receivable financing requires zero collateral. So, no need to pawn your diamond engagement ring or remortgage your house - pretty cool, isn't it!

Factoring does not impact your business's credit score because it is a transaction that does not involve credit. Nonetheless, it can still build your credit score. Factoring builds your credit score by delivering cash tied up in IOUs, ensuring that you receive instant cash days after issuing the invoice. This transaction can:

- **Give your business excellent payment history:** When customers delay payments, you may find yourself submitting your payments late, and in the process incurring late fees. With the capital obtained quickly from accounts receivable financing, a business can pay its invoices on time; this payment consistency improves business credit
- **Help you access capital without using up all your credit:** Maxing out your credit reduces your score. This is because credit rating is (also) calculated according to the percentage of credit used up. Therefore, using cash from factoring prevents maxing out your credit, and helps maintain a high score. It also helps you not to use other credit cards, another cause for a reduction in credit scores

Being a business owner is not easy. Finding suitable financing that works for your company's unique situation can be a tedious task. Be encouraged, though. With poor business credit or without business credit, you still have financing options available to you.

Conclusion

Developing good spending habits, living within your means, and maintaining a good credit score, is key to leveraging credit in order to generate wealth. According to Lynette Khalfani-Cox, the author of *Perfect Credit: 7 Steps to a Great Credit Rating*, a high credit score means (Khalfani, 2010):

- Creditworthiness
- Faster loan and credit approval
- Better loan amounts and credit limits
- Low-interest rates
- Fewer repayment fees
- Ease in establishing a relationship with recognized vendors

- New clients
- Wealth generation

You can leverage your personal credit to acquire business capital for company growth, while building the credit rating necessary for obtaining jumbo business loans in the future.

Leveraging Other People's Money

In the financial world, OPM or other people's money is a slang term referring to financial leverage. It refers to the borrowed capital used to increase the potential returns, also risks, of an investment. Corporations, as well as individuals both, utilize OPM.

Leveraging an investment with other people's money can be a double-edged sword. If the investment becomes profitable, due to leveraging, the profits are magnified. However, if the investment goes south, then the investor who borrowed OPM can incur steep losses.

Capital structure speaks of a company's mix of equity financing and debt. To determine the best mix of equity and debt financing, many factors are taken into consideration. Using other people's money, aka increasing leverage, can increase a company's tax shield. On the other hand, leverage with OPM can increase the risk of bankruptcy, defaulting, or financial distress costs.

Other People's Money Example

Here's an example that shows the risk-return nature of using other people's money (financial leverage):

An investor has $100 to invest in a security which gains $20 or loses 20% over a year. With a gain of 20%, the investor closes the year with a profit of $20 or, $120. If the investment loses 20%, the investor will close the year with a $20 loss, or $80. Compared to the originally invested capital, the gains and losses are reasonable.

Let us now examine a similar investment, with the investor using OPM as financial leverage.

The same investor borrows $400, adds his original $100, and invests the sum of $500 in the same security. That investment will either go up 20% or down 20% by the end of the year. If it gains 20%, the year ends with the investor having $600, a 100% profit of the original $100. If it loses 20%, the investor will suffer a loss of $100, and end up with $400. The investor will have lost 100% of his originally invested capital.

Financial leverage, or using other people's money, dramatically increases the upside gains and downside losses of any investment.

Scaling Other People's Money to Become Wealthy

From the example above, you've seen that there are two ways of getting wealthy; with your own money or with OPM (other people's money). OPM requires high financial intelligence to invest and provides huge returns while creating an incredible velocity of money. Alternatively, using one's own money requires a bit of financial knowledge and provides modest gains.

Which investment method do you prefer?

Other People's Money and Good Debt

You can increase your ROI (Return on Investment) dramatically, by using both OPM and good debt – you can also achieve infinite returns.

OPM is good debt, a loan - to be clear, a good debt gives you money, while a bad debt takes away money. A personal car loan is a bad debt because a car doesn't generate income and depreciates as soon as you purchase it. By contrast, good debt is, for example, an investment property loan. A rental property pays its expenses, including mortgage (or debt service), while generating monthly cash inflows. Therefore, the exception to the vehicle analogy is, say, a car purchased to be used as a rental (car hire) or cab (Uber, etc.).

One negative aspect of good debt is that you can only borrow a percentage of an assets purchase price. In real estate, that would be around 70-80% of the purchase price.

For example, to purchase a $100,000 property, you can only borrow $70,000 to $80,000 from a traditional financial institution, which means that you must raise the balance from other sources.

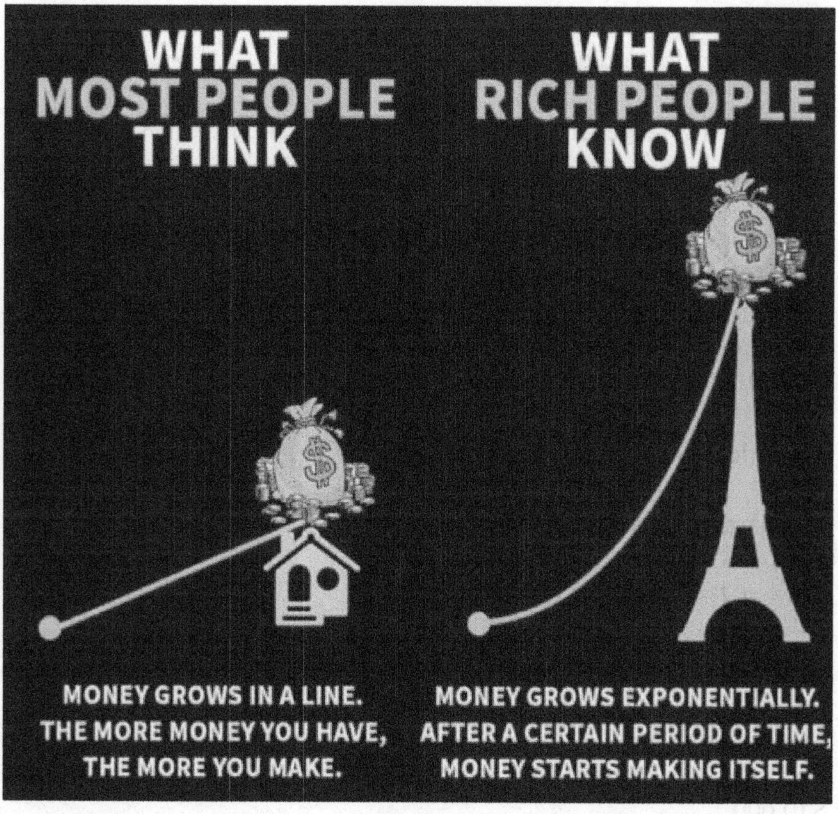

A Higher ROI from Other People's Money

For this reason, you have two choices when presented with a worthy investment: above and beyond the loan, use your own money, or use OPM for the required equity.
To depict the above, here are a few real estate scenarios:

Scenario 1:

Purchase price: $100,000
Loan at 5% interest: $80,000
Own money for equity: $20,000

A simple mortgage calculator reveals an annual cost of $8,500 for the loan

Assuming property income of $11,000 per annum, after expenses are paid, total net income will be $2,500 (i.e. $11,000 – $8,500).

Therefore, ROI for this property would be:
$2,500/$20,000= 12.5%.

Scenario 2:

Purchase price: $100,000
Loan at 5% interest: $80,000
OPM at 7% interest: $20,000

As the chief deal maker, you are paid a net operating income of 50%.

In this arrangement, annual loan costs would be $8,500 with an additional OPM cost of $1,500 (with 7% interest). OPM total costs will be $10,000.

Assuming property income of $11,000 per annum, after expenses are paid, total net income will be $1,000 (i.e. $11,000 – $10,000).

Because you organized the deal, your fee would be, 50% of the NOI (net operating income), which is $500 (50% x $1,000).

Your ROI would be infinite because you are earning $500 without putting any money into the deal.
The above numbers, compared to the real world of investment, are small. When dealing with real-world numbers, you can make massive and infinite returns. You can also suffer enormous losses. High financial intelligence is a requirement if you are going to dapple with other people's money.

Who Gives Away Their Money?

Most people do not have the time to find good deals. They instead rely on well-educated people who have the required skill set to find these deals for them. For instance, a real estate investment advisor will look for suitable apartment buildings, conduct due diligence, negotiate with lenders and owners, and handle project management. In return, ordinary folk line up, hoping to invest with her. Alternatively, the real estate advisor may have a specific criterion on the preferred investor, e.g. one with the ability to invest $1,000,000 per project.

Anyone can carry out investment projects with OPM by teaming up with work-mates, friends, family, and perfect strangers. Be cautious about your investment plans because you don't want to end up in jail!

How to Raise Capital (OPM)

An investor who has built their empire through their savings is laudable. However, I implore you, look beyond the limitations of your resources, and find sources of money elsewhere. Limiting yourself to your wallet and traditional lending is the embodiment of laziness!

Don't worry, here's the cure for you.

First, recognize that it takes creativity and thinking to use other people's money. It requires discipline and intelligence to get other people's money, invest it, and grow it. Not everyone can manage that. It also takes a good reputation, skills, strategies, and persuasion to get someone, even a good friend, to trust you with their hard-earned money. Good news, there is plenty of information out there, and you can learn how to do so. Lenders and investors want to be assured that they will receive a healthy return on their investment. No-one invests their own money to incur losses. So, trust me, no-one will give you their money to make a loss.

Raising funds from other people will require you to address four factors, which will demonstrate the ROI that they seek:

1. **Project:** The lender will be providing capital for what project? Why is the opportunity attractive and unique? Share the vision of the project in its entirety, communicating both pros and cons, and how you plan to overcome the negative aspects of the project.

2. **Partners:** Who are your partners? Key players? Who is organizing the deal and their track record? List comprehensively the experience of each partner and what they bring to the table. Their expertise and network are as much a part of the equation - just as their money is.

3. **Financing:** Reveal the financial plans of the project. Provide details of how the project will make money - be it an investment or business deal. Be realistic and discuss potential problems and roadblocks. Show the amount being raised, how it was, or, will be raised, the sources of the funding, e.g., traditional lenders, private parties, etc., terms and conditions of the borrowed amount, and the allocation of the money.

   Most importantly, reveal in detail the expected ROI and the date when it will be disbursed. Your financing structure and terms must be attractive, to entice potential investors.

Please note: Do not at any point disclose that the money will be used to pay your salary! Investors will feel as though you are taking them for a ride.

4. **Management:** Explain your day-to-day operations and disclose who makes up the management team behind the project. This information is crucial to the continued success of any business venture. Reveal their identities, background, personalities, and ability to work under pressure, etc.

Raising capital should not necessarily be a complicated affair. Ensure that your pitch to your investors is concise and straightforward. If you can clearly communicate the above four points, you are well on your way to securing the financing that you need!

Be careful to deliver on all your promises; future projects rely on the success of initial projects!

Be diligent, increase your financial knowledge, work hard, master the fundamentals of OPM and good debt, and you'll most certainly become wealthy.

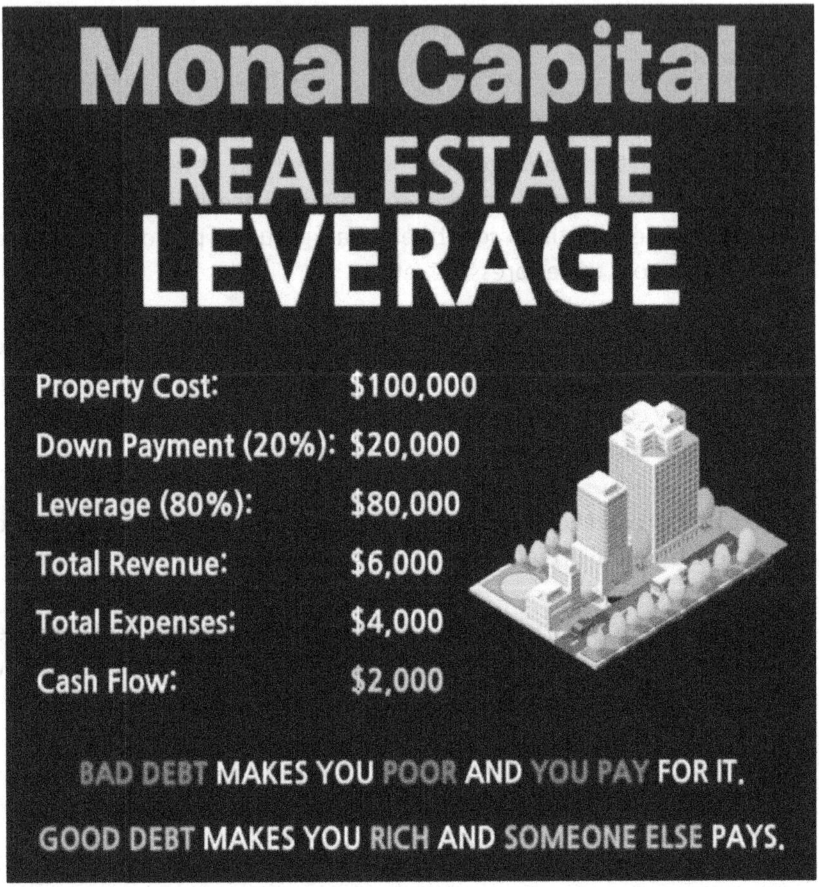
Monal Capital
REAL ESTATE
LEVERAGE
Property Cost: $100,000
Down Payment (20%): $20,000
Leverage (80%): $80,000
Total Revenue: $6,000
Total Expenses: $4,000
Cash Flow: $2,000
BAD DEBT MAKES YOU POOR AND YOU PAY FOR IT.
GOOD DEBT MAKES YOU RICH AND SOMEONE ELSE PAYS.

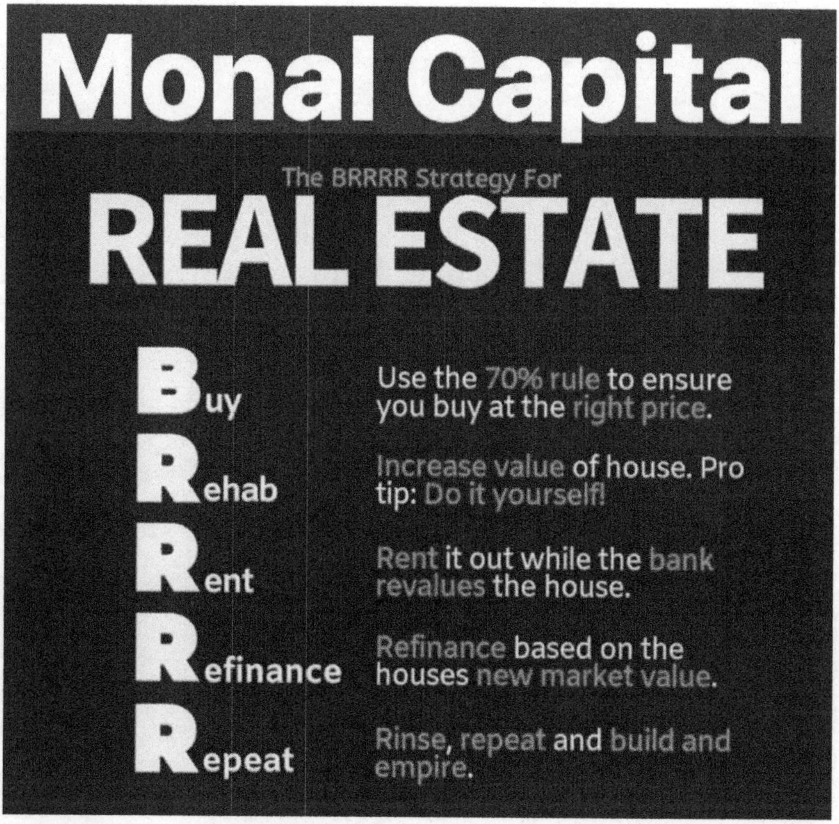
Monal Capital
The BRRRR Strategy For
REAL ESTATE
Buy
Use the 70% rule to ensure you buy at the right price.
Rehab
Increase value of house. Pro tip: Do it yourself!
Rent
Rent it out while the bank revalues the house.
Refinance
Refinance based on the houses new market value.
Repeat
Rinse, repeat and build and empire.

CHAPTER 3

Cashflow and Taxes

CASHFLOW AND TAXES

Cashflow Is King! Money Is Useless Unless It Is Used.

To become successful, you must control the direction of your cashflow. You must understand how to read a financial statement, managing your income and expenses and labeling your assets and liabilities and most importantly making proper investments.

Take Control of your Finances

You should have received a print out of your own personal financial statement with my book. For you to obtain financial freedom, you must first know how to read a statement and control your cashflow

Financial Institutions

Do you ever wonder what happens to your money when is sits in the bank? It loses value. You're losing money why is that? It's something we call inflation- when the value of a dollar decreases and the price of living increases. If you're not saving money to invest your money, you're losing money.

One of the greatest investments that will bring you great cashflow is real estate. Purchase an income producing property creates a positive cashflow. For example, you only need 300K to buy $1 million worth of real estate. It sounds ludicrous doesn't it? Let me explain:

In most scenarios you only need 20% down for a loan if you choose the right property. If you choose the correct property you would immediately have positive cashflow which will pay back the loan and give you a small payout, which is considered passive income. Your unit expenses would be covered by the monthly passive income. Now let's celebrate you are now a real estate investor!!

American Financial Worries

Being rich and successful requires life changing decision making. If you want to be rich and successful you must do what the rich and successful do, and you also must think the way the rich and successful think.

The Importance of Cashflow

Are you worried about your financial future?

According to a 2018 Northwestern Mutual Planning and Progress study, 44% of Americans worry about money more than anything else (Northwestern Mutual, 2018). A 2018 Financial Security Index survey by Bankrate states that in the course of a year, 34% of Americans experienced a significant unplanned expense. Of that group, only 39% of the respondents said that they could cover a $1,000 setback with their savings (Tepper, 2018). A different 2018 Gallup poll reveals that 58% of Americans worry about not having enough money to retire at 65 (Saad, 2018).

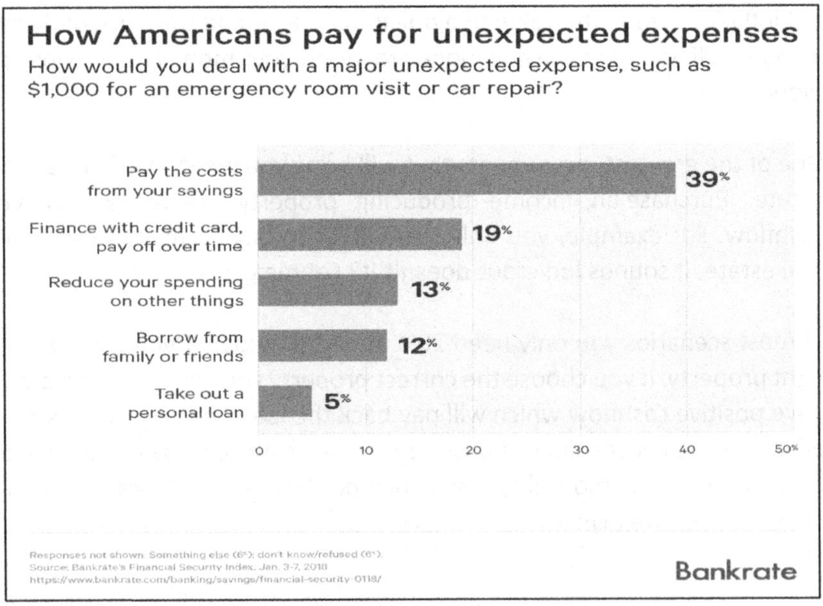

Image Source: Tepper, *Bankrate.com*, 18 Jan 2018

	Very/Moderately worried	Not too/Not at all worried
	%	%
Not being able to pay medical costs in the event of a serious illness or accident	58	41
Not having enough money for retirement	58	39
Not being able to pay medical costs for normal healthcare	44	53
Not being able to maintain the standard of living you enjoy	43	56
Not having enough money to pay for your children's college	37	32
Not having enough to pay your normal monthly bills	34	65
Not being able to pay your rent, mortgage or other housing costs	30	66
Not being able to make the minimum payments on your credit cards	18	64
GALLUP, APRIL 2-11, 2018		

Image Source: Saad, *Gallup.com*, 3 May 2018

Next, please tell me how concerned you are right now about each of the following financial matters, based on your current financial situation -- are you very worried, moderately worried, not too worried or not worried at all?

All these statistics have one thing in common; most Americans do not know how to reach financial independence. They live from paycheck to paycheck, with nary a savings plan, working their butts off, all the while trapped in a vicious cycle of credit card debt.

What a terrifying and depressing position to be in! So how to resolve the situation? Through the powerful concept of cashflow.

What is Cashflow?

The solution to all your financial worries is cashflow. Cashflow is King, while cash is Queen - the reliever of your financial stress and provider of a steady stream of income!

When thinking about the world of investing, there are two reasons why people invest: for cashflow and capital gains.

The main difference between cashflow and capital gains is:

- Cashflow: Cashflow is the steady and ongoing stream of income that you get from a particular investment. This money may be received weekly, monthly, quarterly, or annually, depending on the type of investment. With cashflow, the strategy is to buy and retain, whereas, with capital gains, the plan is to buy and sell.

  In the instance of the stock market, let's imagine that you buy stocks that pay you a dividend each year. That dividend is referred to as cashflow.

  If you become a venture capitalist and invest in start-ups, by giving them loans, you receive a return on your investment. Depending on the agreed terms, every month you may receive interest on the loan from the start-ups. The interest paid is cashflow.

- Capital Gains is the profit you make when you sell an investment. It is a one-time profit that does not recur.

  For example, you buy seven shares of stock for a total of $1,000. The shares go up and are valued at $1,500. You sell your shares. The $500 that you earn from the sale is called capital gains.
  While investing in real estate, you purchase a house for $150,000. You carry out $10,000 renovations and sell it at $200,000. You make a $40,000 profit, or capital gains, on the sale of the house.

  You must sell an asset to be able to realize capital gains.

  On the flip side, if on selling an asset, you lose money - by selling it at less than its purchase price, it is referred to as incurring a capital loss.

Capital gains assume an up-trending market or appreciating market. Capital loss assumes a down-trending or depreciating market.
It goes without saying that to make a profit, the value of the asset must go up. A buyer must pay you more for the asset - than what you paid when purchasing, factoring all associated expenses since purchase.

Cashflow in Business

Cashflow matters to an entrepreneur. It is crucial for a businessperson to understand what cashflow is, how cashflow impacts one's business, and how to manage their businesses cashflow.

In entrepreneurial terms, cashflow is defined as the "in and out" movement of money in a business.

Think of this: Every transaction in your company's bank account is represented as cashflow. Positive cashflow is when your account has more than the required amount (of money) to pay bills and cover other business expenses. A cashflow issue occurs when cash flowing out of your company (expenses), exceeds the cash flowing into your business, i.e., income and revenues.

Cashflow and Investments

There are three main spheres of investment, i.e., real estate, business, or paper assets (stock market).

Cashflow is realized differently in the three industries:

a. **Real Estate Investment.**
   In the real estate market, cashflow investing is what most purchase-and-retain investors pursue.

   For example, you purchase a 10-unit apartment and rent out each unit. On a monthly basis, you collect rent and pay the mortgage and operating expenses. With proper property management, you'll have positive cashflow. Alternatively, with poor management, you'll end up with negative cashflow, thereby necessitating a strong financial foundation to generate positive cashflow.

b. **Entrepreneurship**

In business, cashflow comes from, e.g., customer payments, loans, start-up capital from angel investors, interest on savings, or other investments.

For example, a T-shirt printer will purchase at wholesale price, 1000 plain white cotton T-shirts at $3 each. He will then proceed to print original graphic designs on the shirt and sell each T-shirt at $25. Assuming printing and other company expenses of $10, he makes a profit of $12 per T-shirt. So, due to this profit from T-shirt sales, the printing company has a positive cashflow of $12.

Please note, profit and cashflow are different. Cashflow assumes that cash has already been received, whereas profit must take into consideration a company's financial position in its entirety. Therefore, a business must implement an efficient cashflow management system, which accurately details and accounts for point-of-sale payments, delayed payments, raw materials or stock, salaries, rent, and other operating expenses.

With positive cashflow, a business can run smoothly. High positive cashflow will allow for expansion and new investments. On the other hand, negative cashflow will need to be managed. Please note, most new businesses have a negative cashflow for the first year.

c. **Stock Market**

Investing in the stock market, unlike in real estate and business, is the riskiest of the three approaches. You can invest in the stock market for both capital gains and cashflow. Two methods to follow when investing in stock, with cashflow in mind, are covered calls and dividends. Covered calls (stock options) entail a promise to sell, for a specified duration, in exchange for a premium (income).

Dividends are a percentage of profits paid by companies to shareholders. In most companies, dividends are distributed quarterly or annually.

For example, in a particular quarter of the year, a company declares a $0.50 dividend. A shareholder with 100 shares will receive $50. A profitable quarter and a substantial investment will ensure good returns for an investor and vice versa – a quarter that realizes a loss will mean that an investor will receive reduced dividend amounts.

Why Is Cashflow Important?

Cashflow investing has numerous advantages, namely:

1. **Financial freedom**
   At the mention of financial independence, most people conjure up thoughts of having millions of dollars in savings, or if nothing else, hundreds of thousands of dollars. You do not need to have savings to the tune of hundreds of thousands or millions of dollars to be deemed financially free. You just need your living expenses to be less than your cashflow. To put it a different way, your monthly cashflow (income and revenue) must be significantly more than your expenses.

2. **Worry-free retirement**
   One major advantage of having cashflow as an investment plan is that it eradicates the fear of running out of money. Most folks plan their retirement with the constant concern, being, that they are going to outlive their retirement funds. Assets which provide a monthly cashflow will enable you to have money coming in every month.

3. **Control**
   Invest in what interests you, which you can control. Unlike stock trading and house flipping, having rental properties/business is simple to manage and control. Stock market trading comes with its highs and lows, with a continually fluctuating market environment.

Similarly, the real estate market can have highs or lows, depending on several variables. So, you risk each time you buy a property with the sole intention of flipping it and reselling. Those that have lost their fortunes due to a real estate or stock market crash can attest to this.

Carefully assess what arena to invest in, to get your cashflow started. All things considered; a diversified investment portfolio is advisable.

Exit the Rat Race

Genuine wealth is not calculated in terms of money; cents and dollars. True wealth is measured in terms of time - when you never have to work again because your assets have produced enough positive cashflow to cover all your expenses.

Therefore, financial freedom also describes when your schedule is cleared up, enabling you to spend your time as you please, because your life is no longer controlled by money constraints.

Exiting life's rat race requires you to understand how to get positive cashflow from your assets.

To become financially free even wealthy, your assets, be them you're your businesses, real estate or paper assets, will work around the clock making you money.

What future do you envision for yourself? What changes in your lifestyle do you foresee? If you are one of the 44% of Americans who are stressed about money, perhaps a financial strategy that generates positive cashflow may bring you the relief and peace of mind that you desire.

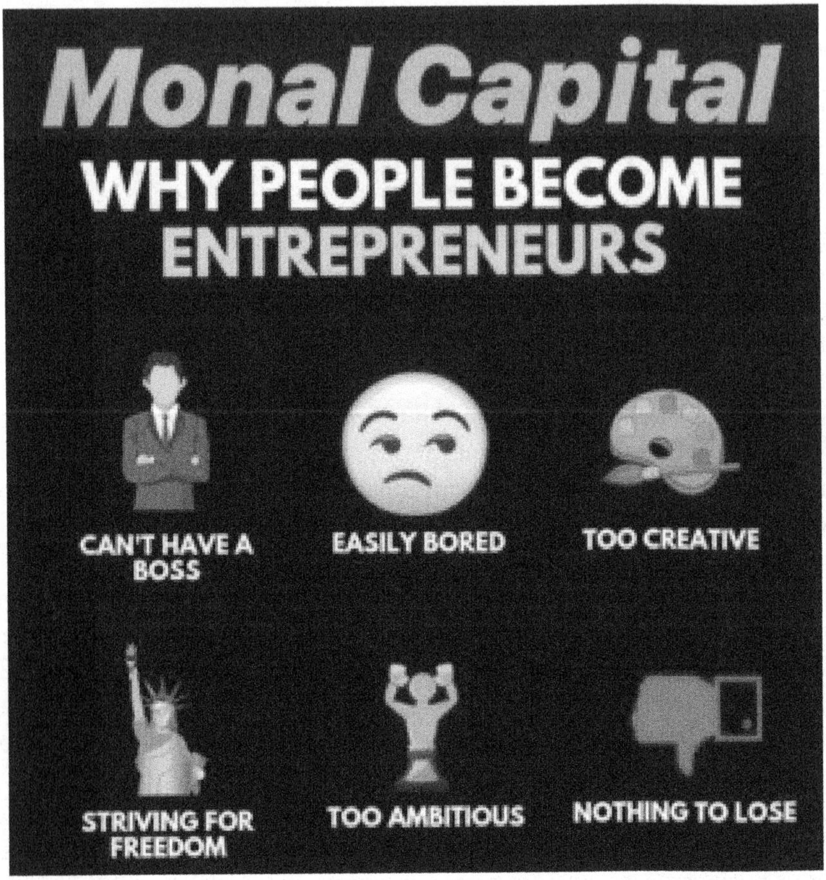

Building Monthly Cashflow

The premise of having cash is that it affords you with buying power. Access to readily available cash provides you with protection against foreclosures or loan defaults. Cashflow is different from having cash in that it shows the ongoing ability to make and use money. Cashflow in accounting describes the relationship between money flowing into your business and money flowing out of it.

You must reduce expenses and increase revenue to generate positive cashflow.

Why Build Monthly Cashflow?

When one borrows money to buy equipment, buildings, and inventory, you are essentially using future cashflow to make your present purchases possible. Therefore, to pay off your debt commitments, you will need to have positive future cashflow. Most companies run their businesses with both short-term credit from vendors and long term-loans from financial institutions or private lenders. The required monthly payments will invariably restrict your free cashflow, slowing down your ability to reinvest in your business.

So, alongside debt management, having strong cashflow provides a business with the capabilities to grow and focus on company expansion, e.g., improving technology, increasing assets, renovating infrastructure, purchasing assets, etc. Positioning your company to have excess cash inflow, helps you face the future proactively and strategically, instead of reactively and defensively.

Cashflow gives your company added flexibility in making critical decisions and responding to emergencies. Stable cashflow allows you to disburse money as dividends to owners and shareholders, strengthening the bond between the owners and the company.

Steady monthly positive cashflow makes you appealing to lenders and gives you the ability to offer attractive credit terms which will garner you, new clients.

Plan Well and Get Organized

So how can one build monthly cashflow?

Whether you dabble in the stock market, real estate, or have a myriad of entrepreneurial ventures, the following cashflow tips will help you get started.

Two main things drive positive cashflow: planning and organization. Let's start at the top. Begin by examining the available cash - which may comprise of money in the company bank account, business loans, personal funds invested into the business, or startup capital from a partner.

Improve Cash In-Flow for businesses

Positive cashflow can be realized with creative marketing, increased sales, and price restructuring. Meticulous planning is also required, especially if your customers have a liberal payment time frame, from the receipt of an invoice to the date of submission of payment.

Implement the following steps to encourage faster cash inflow:

- Promptly issue invoices and regularly follow up on them. This may sound simple enough, but you'll find that some people postpone or avoid paying their bills because they don't want to part with their money.
- Offer an enticing discount for early payment. If your contract has a payment term of 30-days, give a discount for payments made within ten days.
- Require upfront deposits, and for long term projects, schedule milestones with payment intervals for the duration of the project. This will ensure that you earn cash, even while implementing the project.
- Raising your prices may sound counter-intuitive but is one way you can increase or maintain your monthly positive cash inflow. Don't worry about losing previous clients due to price hikes; this strategy will require you to implement the new pricing structure only with new clients while maintaining original pricing with old clients. Alternatively, introducing a premium product will justify higher prices. Bundled products which offer convenience and value are usually fast movers. Always buy low and sell high, to ensure profits and not losses.

- Implement seasonal holiday sales and create unique projects which bring in income. Be creative with pricing options, e.g., encouraging preorders and advance payment.
- Improving efficiency, company productivity, and reducing wastage are surefire ways of reducing cash outflow, which in turn leads to an increase in positive cashflow. Repetitive office tasks should be automated where possible or at least streamlined, to ensure that your staff focuses on revenue generation more than anything else.

Budget well and carefully map money allocation to minimize waste. Strict budget implementation will help prevent wastage and keep expenses lower than revenue. Customer billing is one of those repetitive tasks that can be automated. Streamlining other processes such as client communication, assembling widgets, processing returns, etc. can also increase efficiency. Sell old inventory and unwanted equipment.

Pay Your Bills Cleverly

Due bills must be paid; there are no two ways around it. Paying off bills promptly will help you build a good relationship with your creditors and maintain a good credit score. Besides, it's good manners to do so.

Considering the need to have positive cashflow, you'll need to be smart with your company's outflows when it comes to bill payments:

- Utilize the payment term to the fullest. This is contrary to the advice given above because you are on the customer side of bill repayment. Use the entire payment term to accumulate cash and observe your cashflow. Delaying payment will augur well for your cashflow, as compared to mailing out a check the same day you receive the invoice
- On the flip side, enquire if there any discounts for early payment. (You may be seeing a trend now).
- When making a deal enquire from your vendor if they can offer you flexible payment terms. Be cautious with new deals though - asking for flexible payment can raise suspicion and cause a deal to fall

through. However, if you don't ask for one, you'll never know the response. A payment plan can help you out in a slow business season.

- Set up ETF payments. Automatic scheduling of payment is the most convenient method of paying bills when due, and not a moment sooner. Scheduling also allows you to prepare for payment, thereby ensuring that you will have the funds available.
- Establish genuine relationships with your vendors. A good relationship goes a long way and suppliers are known to provide a line of credit or payment extension to business people that they trust.

Surviving Lean Months

During those lean months, when there is a lag between sales made and receipt of payment, your bills don't magically disappear. Neither do your bills have altered due dates to reflect your lean season.

During the dry seasons, you need cash to keep your business afloat.

Build up cash reserves to alleviate or altogether avoid this problem. By reviewing your cashflow, you can estimate the cash reserves needed to cover your business expenses for a third of a year, half a year, up to one year.

Being aware of these numbers can guide you into making better business decisions.

When you're flush with cash, it is good to contact your bank to organize a line of credit. Interestingly, it is much easier to get money from a bank when you have money than when you don't. Go figure.

The success of your business depends entirely on positive cashflow. Try to leave money over at the end of every month. Extra money is what allows your company to expand and to be considered a reasonable risk by financial institutions. Positive cashflow also frees you up to support community projects while continuing to generate funds to manage your business.
A healthy company has strong monthly positive cash inflows.

Taxes

How To Avoid Paying Taxes (Legally)

Your largest debt is none other than Uncle Sam (IRS). Paying your TAXES which is roughly 30-40% of your gross income which is nearly half of your income. Seems unfair, but it's the law. How do you get out of paying taxes illegally? Simple. Start a business.

Businesses get huge tax breaks. Where employees pay a higher percentage in taxes than the business do!!

The rich pay little to no taxes. Why? Because the rich uses investment such as insurance and real estate to increase their income and protect their money. Another advantage is tax write-offs, where they're writing off their company expenses at the duration of the year. Amazon paid zero in taxes from profits in 2018. Facebook paid $0 in taxes from profits in 2018. Both of these companies made billions of dollars during that tax year.

The rich don't pay taxes legally and this is how! On average employees pay at least 40% in taxes. Small businesses pay at least 60% in taxes. Typically, big businesses pay 20% in taxes and as an investor you pay 0% in taxes.

Why do employees pay 40% in taxes? Why do investors pay zero in taxes? You have to understand the government wants investors to create housing. They want commercial properties built. They want new technology created. So they give the investors incentives because investors are producers who help the economy.

Secret: The more of an asset you become to the government the less you pay in taxes!

For example, you see a company like McDonald's. At first glance you would think McDonald's is in the hamburger business. But in all actuality, they're in the real estate business. McDonald businesses produces enough income to buy the real estate in which it is built on!

How taxes can work for you?

Three terms the rich use when approaching taxes:

a. **Amortization**: the action or process of gradually writing off the initial cost of an asset or just paying down debt with your business earnings

b. **Appreciation**: in general terms, is an increase in the value of an asset over time. When your real estate property goes up in value it's appreciated

c. **Depreciation**: a reduction in the value of an asset with the passage of time, due in particular to wear and tear. It is another deduction for tax purposes, but it's no money coming out your pocket. So what's really happening is you're lowering your taxes and because you're paying depreciation your cashflow increases.

CHAPTER 4

Assets and Liabilities

ASSETS AND LIABILITIES

Making Money or Losing It!

Anything that puts money in your pocket is considered an asset. Anything that takes money out of your pocket is considered a liability. Simple as this may seem a lot of people still get this misconstrued.

Anyone looking to start a business needs to get very familiar with the concepts of assets, liabilities, revenue, and expenses. Think of your business as a living organism and those elements as its vital signs. Assets and liabilities are the fundamental elements of your company's financial position. Revenue and expenses represent the cashflow of your company's operations.

For example, many people say the purchase of their first home is considered their most valuable asset. Building equity in the home increases the value of the home. But more importantly, is that home putting money in your pocket on a monthly basis, or is that home taking money out of your pocket monthly?

Consequently, buying a home for yourself is not necessarily an asset unless you rent the rooms out in that home and your tenants pay your mortgage and upkeep and you create a positive cashflow!

Assets Versus Liabilities

Every business is composed of assets and liabilities. Though different in nature, the purpose of these two components is to increase the life and efficiency of a business. Accounting defines assets as things that provide present and future benefit to a business. That's the reason companies are encouraged to reduce expenses and build assets.

The simplest definition of liabilities is; things that you must pay off in the immediate or distant future. Obligations (liabilities) are created when you receive funds, services, or a product with the expectation that you'll pay them off later. Simply put: anything that takes money out of your pockets is considered a liability.

What are Assets?

An asset is any tangible (real) or intangible resource owned by a business (or individual), which can be owned or controlled, to create positive economic value. Assets can produce value for years.

For example, if you purchased two metal filing cabinets for your office. The cabinets have a lifetime value of 25 years. That means your metal filing cabinets will provide you value (filing office documents), which will enable you to get paid for 25 years.

That's a simple example. A more sophisticated example of an asset would be real estate, e.g. rental apartments.

An item is an asset if it can be exchanged for cash. Certain assets can give you direct cash inflow, while others provide in kind. The metal cabinets provide 25 years of storage and convenience by helping you keep important company documents. Simply, anything that puts money in your pockets is considered an asset.

Another type of asset is investments. Companies can invest money into bonds, equities, and other investment instruments, with the intention of earning interest on their money. Investments are categorized as assets due to their ability to generate direct cash inflows.

Types of Assets

There are two categories of assets, namely current assets and non-current assets, which are further subdivided into tangible and intangible assets.

a. **Current Assets**

Current assets are assets that can be liquidated within 12 months. Current assets include; cash, cash equivalents, inventories, prepaid expenses, short-term investments, prepayments and accrued income, current income tax assets, foreign currency, trade and other receivables, derivative assets and assets held for sale.

b. **Non-Current Assets**

Non-current assets also referred to as fixed assets, are assets that cannot be liquidated into cash immediately. Though immediate conversion into cash is not possible, fixed assets provide a company economic benefits in the long run.

Non-current assets include; property, plant (factory), equipment, goodwill, investments in associates and joint ventures, intangible assets, employee benefits assets, financial assets, and deferred tax assets.

c. **Tangible Assets**

Tangible assets, or real assets, are those that exist physically, i.e., can be touched. A real asset derives its value from its physical qualities. Real assets can either be natural substances, or man-made ones. Tangible assets include; Cash, land, gold, oil, buildings, plant and machinery, equipment, and inventories.

Real assets and financial assets are lumped together as tangible assets by the Internal Revenue Service (IRS), though they are separate and distinct from each other. Financial assets are liquid properties that derive their value from an underlying asset or a contractual claim. They can be either physical, e.g., cash or a bond certificate or intangible (not physical), e.g., mutual fund or money market account.

d. **Intangible Assets**
   Intangible assets are those that do not exist physically, i.e., cannot be touched. They include; goodwill, copyright, trademark, patent, etc.

e. **Fictitious Assets**
   Fictitious assets are not assets; they are instead losses or expenses that could not be written off during a calendar year. Fictitious or fake assets include; promotional costs, discount allowed on the issue of shares, preliminary expenses, loss on issue of debentures, etc.

Valuation of Assets

Assets undergo valuation for the purpose of mergers and acquisitions, capital budgeting, and investment analysis. When investing, an organization is responsible for calculating the value of tangible assets, e.g., buildings and intangible assets, e.g., trademarks and patents. Asset appraisal is the only method available to a company to establish the current and projected (future) value of an investment.

There are four ways in which a company can value its assets:

1. **Absolute Value Method:** With the absolute value method, the present or current value of assets is ascertained. The two models used are; Gordon model (single period) and DCF Valuation method (multi-periods)
2. **Relative Value Method:** With the relative value method, similar assets are compared, and thereafter the assets values are determined
3. **Option Pricing Model:** With this model, certain types of assets are valued, e.g., employee stock options, warrants, etc.
4. **Fair Value Method:** According to US GAAP (FAS 157), the assets should be sold off or purchased only at their fair value

What are Liabilities?

A liability is an obligation or, something owed to someone else. Liabilities are an organization's legal financial debts or, obligations that occur during business operations. Liabilities can be either limited or unlimited.

Limited liability means that the business owner will not incur personal financial risk for any organizational debt. Unlimited liability means that the business owner will be held liable for any company debts. Hence, the reason why entrepreneurs are advised to form Limited Liability Companies (LLC) instead of sole proprietorships.

Liabilities are paid over-time via the transfer of a myriad of economic benefits, including but not limited to, money, goods, or services. They include; loans, mortgages, accounts payable, accrued expenses, and deferred revenues.

Liabilities are either long term, that is, paid (concluded) after a year, or short term, i.e., concluded within a year.

For example, if an organization takes a loan from a financial institution, the loan would be the company's liability. Another example is, if a gemstone vendor sells diamonds to a jeweler, and invoices the jewelry store. The outstanding amount that the jewelry store owes to the supplier is a liability.

The assumption made about a liability is that it will provide economic benefit in the future. Most companies get involved with liabilities because they need assistance to sustain existing business operations or to expand.

Types of Liabilities

The two main types of liabilities are referred to as current and non-current, depending on the context.

a. **Current Liabilities**
These are short-term liabilities which can be paid within a year. They include; provisions, financial debt (short term), trade and other payables, current income tax liabilities, accruals and deferred revenue income, accounts payable, interests payable, current maturities of long-term debt, customer deposits in advance, derivative liabilities, sales taxes payable, short term loans and liabilities directly associated with assets held for sale.

b. **Non-Current Liabilities**
Non-current liabilities are also called long-term liabilities. These are liabilities that can be paid off over a long time. They include; provisions, financial debt (long term), employee benefits liability, deferred tax liabilities, and other payables.

Leverage and Liabilities

A company is viewed as leveraged when it takes a loan (liability) from a financial institution to acquire new assets. Companies are advised to have a good debt to equity ratio to encourage company efficiency and growth. Too much debt is harmful, while a 40% debt to 60% equity ratio is ideal. Debt that is more than 40% should be reduced.

Comparison: Assets Versus Liabilities

The most important differences between assets and liabilities are:

- Assets are the things that will pay off the company for a short or long period of time. On the other hand, liabilities are obligations owed by the company for either a short or long period of time. Obligations that are used to acquire assets create leverage for a business.
- On the balance sheet, assets, when increased, are debited and when decreased, credited. Liabilities, when increased, are credited and when decreased are debited.
- Fixed assets become depreciated. This means that over time, due to wear and tear, they lose their value. Land is the only asset that does not depreciate. Liabilities do not depreciate but are instead paid off during a specified period (short or long term).

- Assets assist in cashflow generation for businesses. Liabilities cause cash outflow because obligations must be paid off. Liabilities are different from expenses.
- Assets are acquired to increase efficiency and to expand a business. Liabilities are incurred when assets are acquired, with the motive being a reduction in future liabilities.

Conclusion

Assets and liabilities are part of the business package. A business cannot perpetuate itself without creating assets. At the same time, without liability, a company cannot generate leverage for itself.

A business will thrive if liabilities are taken only for the purpose of acquiring assets, and if assets are wisely utilized. With that said, due to the uncontrollable factors surrounding entrepreneurship, e.g., recession, success is not guaranteed. It is advisable for a business to invest in assets which generate cashflow from a variety of sources.

The secret to wealth building is to have a diversified business portfolio featuring multiple streams of income. Diversification is necessary to overcome unprecedented events in the business world.

Income Producing Assets

The number one key to becoming wealthy is building multiple streams of income.

The author of *Rich Habits*, Tom Corley studied 233 wealthy individuals and discovered that a good number of self-made millionaires got wealthy from multiple streams of income (Corley, 2010). Of the 233 individuals:

- 65% had three streams of income
- 45% had four streams of income
- 29% had five or more streams of income

The most compelling reason to have multiple streams of income is security – if one stream fails to turn a profit, or is negatively affected in some other way, having more than one income option will keep you going.

Ways to Create Multiple Streams of Income

Implement the following tips to create multiple streams of income:

1. **Save:** Strive to save 10%-20% of your net income per year
2. **Study:** Learn new skills and acquire knowledge that will help you invest intelligently and start up a side business

3. **Invest:** Invest in a company that will generate income
4. **Reinvest:** From the profits of the first business, reinvest in other types of investments, e.g., the stock market or, other assets, e.g., rental property

You can start your own business or partner with others. Regardless of how you plan to do it, just do it!

1. **Savings Accounts**

   Starting a savings account is the most basic and least profitable income-producing asset in the investment world. While offering low-interest rates, having a savings account teaches you the most beneficial financial lesson: financial discipline. By training yourself not to spend money, you learn self-denial and delayed gratification – money lessons that make all the difference between a mediocre earner and a super-wealthy person.

   The trick is not to get stuck at this stage. Move on from this phase and venture into riskier but high yielding investments.

2. **Websites and Online Business**

   Online stores, e.g., Amazon and Shopify, are some of the most convenient online businesses you could have. Amazon FBA (Fulfilled by Amazon) gives you the opportunity to set up an e-commerce store that virtually runs itself, save for minimal input from you.

   Website sales are another way to make money. There's an industry of people who buy and sell websites, e.g., blogs, online company websites, etc. Most online businesses can be purchased, sold, flipped, and traded. The largest website marketplace, flippa.com, is one such site that deals in selling small to mid-sized websites.

   Affiliate marketing, YouTube channels, eBook sales are other types of online businesses that you can conduct, which offer good profits with low overheads.

For example, you can write an eBook about passive income and sell it at $50 per book.

3. **Traditional Businesses**
Traditional businesses, albeit boring, are surprisingly profitable. Most self-made millionaires hone their financial skills with a classic income-producing activity. Consider boosting your portfolio with:

    a. **Laundromats**
    Yes, those rundown laundromats are money makers, believe it or not. Ignoring that they also serve as fronts for those engaged in illicit business, e.g., drug dealing, laundromats are cash cows.

    A laundromat located at a place with good traffic, e.g., low-cost apartments and neighborhoods with college attending youth or young professionals, can earn $46,000 annually. An average-sized laundromat needs only one full-time employee and has minimal overheads.

    b. **Car Washes**
    Self-service car washes (wand or coin-op) have low startup costs, with each bay bringing in monthly revenue of nearly $1,489. A two-bay operation with 10% usage brings in $41,000 in annual revenues. A 2016 U.S. Census Bureau survey reveals that the average in-bay automatic car wash earned an annual profit of $86,531, and a large tunnel/conveyor belt car wash earned annual revenue of $686,250. Startup costs vary from one car wash to another.

    c. **Coffee Shops**
    High-end coffee shops are all the rage, thanks to Starbucks "cool" albeit expensive coffee brand. The average coffee and tea shop spend pennies to brew a cup, yet sells it at $3-$5. Those are wonderful margins for any establishment!

    When investing in a coffee/tea shop, think trendy location, with hipster décor and industrial roasters. A profitable coffee shop is all about attracting the right crowd. Your biggest draw will be ambiance and location, in addition to quality java and delicious snacks

d. **Dive Bars**
Yup, those dingy, poorly lit bars are rewarded for hardly maintaining their facilities by attracting a particular crowd. Think affordable drinks sold at an affordable location

e. **Late Night (aka Post-Clubbing) Food Spots**
These are popular in urban locations, in areas which have nightclubs. New York has these food spots, featuring mile-long food lines at 3 AM. They offer basic fast food, e.g., pizza slices, fried chicken, hotdogs, etc. Think low overheads with high margins

4. **Franchises**

You must have seen the recent viral social media memes about the friendly rivalry surrounding Popeyes and Chick-fil-A's chicken sandwiches. Owning a franchise is one of the more expensive, stress-free, passive income-earning opportunities.

A franchise purchase permits one to use a parent company's trademarks, branding, trade secrets (ingredients, recipes, etc.), and business plan in exchange for an amount of the store's percentage profits. A franchisee outsources day to day operations, which frees up their time while earning them excellent profits.

Be advised that the franchise fees are steep, with McDonald's pegged at $45,000 and initial investment ranging between $1 million to $2.2 million. In addition to steep startup costs, you are required to have $500,000 in liquid assets. An average McDonalds location makes $2.6 million in sales annually.

A more affordable Chick-fil-A has stringent requirements and an incredibly competitive program. Only 0.4% of franchise applicants make the cut. Chick-fil-A has a stipulation that requires owners to be on-site at least 30 hours a week. That pretty much removes "passive income" from the equation.

Subway has a friendlier arrangement that allows absentee ownership. Among the leading fast-food franchises, Subway has the most affordable startup costs of $116,000 to $253,000.

It is my goal and ambition to start a healthy fast-food chain in the near future!

5. **Stock Markets**
   One time-tested investment option is in dividend stocks. While they are not a guaranteed money-maker due to market fluctuations, they are an easy way to generate significant passive income. A straightforward way of investing in dividend stocks is by purchasing low-cost equity, e.g., SPYD, HDY, NOBL, VSDA, SPVD, SPHD, TDIV, LVHI, PGX, and others. Don't bother selecting individual stock – it's safer to buy a dividend ETF for the long haul.

6. **Real Estate**
   Investing in real estate with the motive of earning monthly cashflow is the safer of the investment opportunities and is favored by self-made millionaires such as Robert Kiyosaki, Grant Cardone, and Dean Graziosi.

   a. **Single-Family Rental Houses**
      A classic of rental properties, investing in single-family rental homes is where most investors begin. A single-family rentals entry barrier is low; they're easy to manage and can be a cash machine. Real estate investors start with one house and gradually grow their portfolio.

   b. **Multi-family Rental Properties (i.e., Duplexes, Triplexes, and Quads)**
      In snotty real estate definition (not real world), a rental owner has one property, whereas a landlord is one managing multi-

family rental properties featuring two, three or even four units. Set your real estate investment goals to becoming a full-fledged landlord!

Considering the number of tenants under one roof, multi-family units have an economy of scale that is not possible to arrive at with single-family units. With regards to rental cash inflow, the numbers work that much better when considering multi-family units, as compared to single-family units. It is also easier for a real estate investor to stomach venturing into construction when imagining that one foundation will support two, three, four, and more paying renters.

As a brand-new investor, a well-maintained older apartment unit may be more affordable to purchase, and less stressful to deal with, than a brand new one. It is better to buy an older apartment, due to ready renters, depreciation, and tax discounts. As a newbie investor with limited capital, spread your risk by not purchasing too many units in one location.

The only issue with multi-family properties is the competition surrounding rental property purchases. There's always a scramble for apartment units because of the limited supply - other investors will equally be interested in purchasing apartment units.

c. **Mogul Status- Apartment Buildings**

Big shot and tycoon territory are when you are able to buy or build apartment buildings with ten or more multi-family units. Increasing rent by $20 for a couple of units won't make much difference to your positive cash inflow. Now imagine managing a 12-unit apartment block. The $20 increase creates an additional $3,000 in annual revenue!

d. **Short Term Rentals**

Rentals earn more income as short-term rentals with sites such as VRBO, Airbnb, and other short-stay programs. With these sites, renting out an apartment has become a breeze. Some landlords find that it is more profitable to rent to different people over a short period rather than having one single tenant.

People on holiday/vacation will fork out more money on the higher daily rates, as compared to what a long-term tenant would agree to pay daily.

This arrangement also requires that the apartments are fully serviced, with hospitality, cleaning, and regular maintenance, which sort of stops them from being passive income assets. With competent employees (per number of rentals), you can increase the passive income nature of owning a rental apartment.

The initial investment will be higher due to buying electronics, furniture, toiletries, etc., needed to make it ready for short term occupancy. Short term rentals experience higher levels of wear and tear and also need extra insurance for theft and damage.

e. **Real Estate Crowdsourcing**

If you don't have the amounts required to purchase real estate, don't worry, there's always real estate crowdsourcing. Crowdsourcing allows an individual to acquire a piece (stocks) of a real estate project (commercial or residential). With most commercial or residential projects, you can invest a minimum of $500 and expect annual returns of 7-13%.

These returns are much better than the bond market, CD's, P2P lending, the average private equity, and dividend investing profits. Most importantly, you will have a physical asset, unlike with P2P lending.

Finally, it is vital that you act when interest rates are at rock bottom levels, and while you have the patience and strength. Get your investing started!

Monal Capital
MAKE MONEY WHILE YOU SLEEP
INVESTING
Real Estate Investment Trusts (REITs)
Dividend Stocks
Physical Real Estate (Buy To Let)
Crowd Funded Real Estate
Peer to Peer Lending
INVESTING IDEAS

CHAPTER 5

Generational Wealth

GENERATIONAL WEALTH

Wealth is measured in time, not dollars.

For example, if your expenses are $2,000 per month, and you have savings of $10,000, your wealth amounts to 5 months. Your goal, therefore, is to create a lifetime of self-sustaining wealth.

Wealth transfer to the next generation is part and parcel of financial planning. Some people might be satisfied with saving enough for retirement and leaving a piece of property for their children. Wealthy people, on the other hand, want their money to move from one generation to another.

With their vast financial portfolio of companies and investments, mega-wealthy people have accumulated incredible wealth. If managed wisely, that wealth can benefit several future generations of family members and charitable organizations.

These noble intentions are well and good. However, due to the following culprits, 90% of family fortunes are eroded after the first generation:

- Inflation
- Taxes
- Bad investments
- Natural reduction of assets
- A youthful generation who are not prepared to handle the responsibilities of managing inherited wealth

It requires careful planning to ensure that wealth lasts for generations. In addition to growing their assets, the wealthy learn how to protect their money from inflation, taxes, fees, and potential estate problems. As one becomes wealthier, a person's focus changes from generating wealth to preserving wealth.

Therefore, family legacy discussions and tax estate planning become part of the wealth-building quotient. Lack of planning and a clear road map may mean losing money, sometimes running into the millions of dollars - during the transfer process.

Below are strategies that, if implemented, will ensure that your money will last for generations.

1. **Set Goals**
   Listing your investment goals is key. Articulating the returns you want to see, sets the stage for your investment plans, and the risks that you are prepared to accept.

   To ensure that your money lasts several generations, and to cover the various branches of the family tree, you will need to use different methods to invest, as compared to when transferring money directly to your immediate heirs.

2. **Build a Framework**
   One way that you can make your money last is by putting your assets into a trust. The trustee you choose, be it an individual or a firm, will then advise you on how to invest the money. This can safeguard your wealth from heirs who may make mistakes while investing.

   A bloodline trust is one type of trust, where assets or money can only be inherited by blood relatives. Trusts are protected from divorce or creditors. Assets that are not included as part of a will, but are instead held in trust, can also bypass probate.

   The trust holder can carefully structure parameters around payouts.

For example, the beneficiaries may receive different amounts at different ages, say, 19 and 26. They may also have to reach certain milestones, e.g., complete university or be employed at the family company, to get the stipulated amount. Romantic movie plots will often communicate the requirement to the heir as; get married by a certain age, or you'll lose your inheritance.

In real life, a lawyer experienced with inheritance laws and managing trusts should draft the trust to ensure that the requirements are reasonable and can be enforced. Benefactors would not want their inheritance to cause more harm than good.

3. **Diversify Investments**
Diversification is key to having a mix of assets, which will make up your financial legacy. It is advisable that you achieve a diversified portfolio by putting your money in a variety of industries and geographical sectors.

   While income-producing investments, e.g., bonds, may be sufficient for retirement income, they have a limited value when building a legacy. Focus on continually fine-tuning your asset mix and structure of the estate. Be sure to discuss money matters with your heirs; how to grow, protect, and share it (among heirs).

4. **Guaranteed Products (GIFs)**
Those with moderate-sized nest eggs may find that guaranteed investment funds (GIFs), or segregated fund products – offer the required security.

   Insurance companies sell and manufacture GIFs. They are similar to mutual funds because they offer market-based investments but come with added guarantees because they are insurance contracts. These guarantees provide a guaranteed amount; a guaranteed income, to the contract holder or beneficiaries at either maturity or death.

If you are a risk-averse investor – one who doesn't want to lose money – you may wish to have GIFs featuring in your portfolio. With GIFs, the market value of your investment may go up or down. However, at maturity or death, a portion of the principal amount is guaranteed.

These contracts, because they are insurance-based, offer potential creditor protection that you cannot receive with typical non-registered investment products.

GIFs also offer the added benefit of estate planning. As is the case with life insurance, if you have a named recipient, your death benefit will be directly paid to your beneficiary. The money won't be subject to probate because it won't pass through the estate. The advantage to that is – the settlement remains private, with a quick wealth transfer process, where additional accounting and legal fees are not incurred.

5. **Tax Efficiency**
   Some GIFs contracts provide an income that may enable you to pay less tax. Fewer taxes paid means that more money will be available for your legacy.

   Income paid on non-registered contracts are considered a withdrawal from the GIF contract, so, it is partly taxed as a capital gain and partially as a return of capital. Compared to ordinary income, capital gains are generally taxed at a lower rate. The income payment can help those receiving Old Age Security (OAS), by reducing the "claw back." The government also reduces OAS payments if one's income exceeds a certain amount.

   GIFs may also be structured to create a do-it-yourself pension. Benefit pensions which were enjoyed by previous generations are becoming increasingly rare. A smart retirement savings strategy would be to have a deferred guaranteed income option in a TFSA (Tax-Free Savings Account), while holding a GIF contract. Most families focus on RRSPs (Registered Retirement Savings Plan) or company pensions, which are fully taxable. They also trigger significant tax liabilities upon retirement and at death. Therefore, by receiving a portion of your guaranteed income from a TFSA, you will benefit from tax-free withdrawals as well as tax-sheltered growth.

6. **Wealth Transfer**
Legacy planning, with its available strategies and products, is one thing; family dynamics and relationships is another. Talking about money and inheritance with your family is difficult and requires a delicate and sensitive approach. It is your blessed opportunity to advise them on the legacy being entrusted to them. Strategizing and planning is a two-pronged process; one requires you to personally prepare your family, while the other requires a financial trustee's input.

a. **Personal Preparation**
There are two important principles to implement when preparing your heirs to be good stewards of your legacy.

Principle 1 - The Family's Values, Mission and Unity

Teach your children your family values: what you as an individual believe and therefore, the family in its entirety. What do you as a family support? What do you oppose? What are your family's guiding principles? You can obtain these values from your religion's tenets.

Great wealth is sometimes accompanied by laziness and complacency. Teach your children not to get comfortable; to always be on a mission. Obtaining wealth is not for the sake of being wealthy - money saves lives through the building of homeless shelters, enabling medical research, etc. Owning a large company means that hundreds of family's basic needs are met. Teach your children that money and power should be acquired with the mission being: to alleviate human suffering.

Raise compassionate and loving children who empathize with and mitigate human suffering.
Finally, love your spouse and offspring, your immediate and extended family. Personally demonstrate to your family and all human beings you encounter; love, generosity, self-discipline, good manners, peace, and unity. These lessons will ensure the well-being, love, good health, peace, and safety for all, for generations to come.

Principle 2 - Age-Appropriate Wealth and Financial Management Training

Teach the younger generation critical financial and wealth-generating principles, e.g., saving money, investing, etc. Purchase piggy banks for the little ones. For older children, open savings accounts and buy them age-appropriate financial books. Allocate chores and compensate them for work well done. Teach them about assets and liabilities and how to spend their money. Invest in teaching tools that appeal to their creativity and age group.

Even a little child in kindergarten can clean up after themselves by picking up their toys. They are also financially astute, what with their constantly requesting money to buy candy! Start teaching them about money from a young age.

Invite the older children into the family business; entrust them with light responsibilities. Avoid being pushy or demanding, so that they do not develop an aversion to working with you in the family business.

Steadily reveal to your adult children, financial details about your company's, and investments. Allow them to participate in wealth-generating brainstorming sessions and provide solutions to financial situations, e.g., how to increase cashflow.

Lead them to see themselves as valuable and essential decision-makers. Spend time with them, showing them how to invest in real estate, bonds, the stock market, etc. Teach them the value of strong balance sheets, positive cashflow, etc. Teach your children valuable lessons about the nature of perfect timing when investing, e.g., how to acquire assets affordably, when the economy is struggling.

In other words, teach your generations to be entrepreneurial, innovative, and wise. When they invest wisely, reward them. When they fail, encourage them and give them hope that tomorrow will prove to be a better day.

b. **Hire a Trustee.**

Most wealthy individuals hire trustees (individuals or firms) who cultivate relationships with multiple generations. This is key to lasting loyalty and deepened trust. These family wealth advisors help families remain harmonious and whole after the leader passes away. They spend sufficient amounts of time in preparing your heirs (adults) to inherit wealth, even as they give you investment advice.

Their four-step approach to cultivating a multi-generational legacy plan is by:

1. Understanding your family's dynamics
2. Meeting your children
3. Transforming heirs into clients
4. Implementing legacy plans

Author B. Ray Anderson has a fabulous book on trusts and the IRS entitled, *Trusts You Can Trust* (Anderson, 1998).

CONCLUSION:

In order to ensure the fair, seamless, and peaceful transfer of wealth from one generation to another, now is the time for you to enter legacy discussions. Make your money outlast the generations to come by creating a legacy plan, setting goals, selecting diverse investments, increasing tax efficiency, and obtaining products with guaranteed returns.

My daughter, Mia, and I reading to her class.

Works Cited

WORKS CITED

Anderson, B. Ray and Johnson, F. McKay. *Trusts You Can Trust.* B.R. Anderson. 1998.

Corley, Thomas. *Rich Habits - The Daily Success Habits of Wealthy Individuals*. The Secrets to Financial Success R, Langdon Street Press. 2010.

Hill, Napoleon and Sartwell, Matthew. *Napoleon Hill's Keys to Success: The 17 Principles of Personal Achievement.* TarcherPerigee. 2017.

Hill, Napoleon and Cornwell, Ross. *Think and Grow Rich.* New Holland Publishers. 2019.

Khalfani-Cox, Lynnette. *Perfect Credit: 7 Steps to a Great Credit Rating.* Advantage World Press, 2010.

Kiyosaki, Robert T. *Rich Dad's Cashflow Quadrant: Guide to Financial Freedom*. Plata Publishing. 2011.

"Newsroom | Northwestern Mutual - Planning & Progress Study 2018." *Newsroom | Northwestern Mutual*, news.northwesternmutual.com/planning-and-progress-2018.

Saad, Lydia. "Paying for Medical Crises, Retirement Lead Financial Fears." *Gallup.Com*, 3 May 2018, news.gallup.com/poll/233642/paying-medical-crises-retirement-lead-financial-fears.aspx.

Seligman, Martin. *Authentic Happiness: Using the New Positive Psychology to Realize Your Potential for Lasting Fulfillment.* Nicholas Brealey Publishing, 2017.

Tepper, Taylor. "Most Americans Don't Have Enough Savings To Cover A $1K Emergency | Bankrate.Com." *Bankrate.com*, 18 Jan 2018, www.bankrate.com/banking/savings/financial-security-0118.

Your Personal Financial Statement

PERSONAL FINANCIAL STATEMENT AS OF ______
Date

SUBMITTED TO: ______________________________

PERSONAL INFORMATION	
APPLICANT (NAME)	**CO-APPLICANT (NAME)**
Employer	Employer
Address of Employer	Address of Employer
Business Phone No. / No. of Years with Employer / Title/Position	Business Phone No. / No. of Years with Employer / Title/Position
Name of previous employer & position (if with current employer less than 3 yrs.) / No. of Yrs.	Name of previous employer & position (if with current employer less than 3 yrs.) / No. of Yrs.
Home Address	Home Address
Home Phone No. / Social Security No. / Date of Birth	Home Phone No. / Social Security No. / Date of Birth
Name, Phone No. of your Accountant	Name, Phone No. of your Accountant
Name, Phone No. of your Attorney	Name, Phone No. of your Attorney
Name, Phone No. of your Investment Adviser/Broker	Name, Phone No. of your Investment Advisor/Broker
Name, Phone No. of your Insurance Advisor	Name, Phone No. of your Insurance Advisor

Cash Income & Expenditures Statement For Year Ended ____________ (Omit cents)

ANNUAL INCOME	AMOUNT ($)
Salary (applicant)	$
Salary (co-applicant)	
Bonuses & Commissions (applicant)	
Bonuses & Commissions (co-applicant)	
Rental Income	
Interest Income	
Dividend Income	
Capital Gains	
Partnership Income	
Other Investment Income	
Other Income (List)**	
TOTAL INCOME >	$

ANNUAL EXPENDITURES		AMOUNT ($)
Federal Income and Other Taxes		$
State Income and Other Taxes		$
Rental Payments, Co-op, or Condo Maintenance		
Mortgage Payments	Residential	
	Investment	
Property Taxes	Residential	
	Investment	
Interest & Principal Payments on Loans		
Insurance		
Investments (including tax shelters)		
Alimony/Child Support		
Tuition		
Other Living Expenses		
Medical Expenses		
Other Expense (List)		
TOTAL EXPENDITURES >		$

Any significant changes expected in the next 12 months? ☐ Yes ☐ No (If yes, attach information.)

** Income from alimony, child support, or separate maintenance income need not be revealed if the applicant or co-applicant does not wish to have it considered as a basis for repaying this obligation.

THE FINANCIAL FREEDOM BOOK

Staleon Group
Publications

Made in the USA
Monee, IL
04 November 2026

67378317R00079